First World War
and Army of Occupation
War Diary
France, Belgium and Germany

24 DIVISION
73 Infantry Brigade,
Brigade Machine Gun Company
22 February 1916 - 28 February 1918

WO95/2219/3

The Naval & Military Press Ltd
www.nmarchive.com
Published in association with The National Archives

Published by

The Naval & Military Press Ltd

Unit 10 Ridgewood Industrial Park,

Uckfield, East Sussex,

TN22 5QE England

Tel: +44 (0) 1825 749494

www.naval-military-press.com

www.nmarchive.com

This diary has been reprinted in facsimile from the original. Any imperfections are inevitably reproduced and the quality may fall short of modern type and cartographic standards.

© Crown Copyright
Images reproduced by permission of The National Archives, London, England, 2015.

Contents

Document type	Place/Title	Date From	Date To
Heading	WO95/2219/3		
Heading	73rd Machine Gun Coy Feb 1916-Feb 1918		
Heading	73rd Machine Gun Company. 22nd February to 31st May 1916		
Heading	73rd Machine Gun Company		
Miscellaneous	The D.A.G., 3rd Echelon, The Base.	04/05/1916	04/05/1916
War Diary	Ouderdom	22/02/1916	23/03/1916
War Diary	Court Dreve (Sh 28. T.24a.4.6.)	24/03/1916	06/04/1916
War Diary	Petit Pont Sheet 28 T.22b.27	08/04/1916	30/04/1916
War Diary	Petit Pont	30/04/1916	11/05/1916
Miscellaneous	The D.A.G., 3rd Echelon, The Base	31/05/1916	31/05/1916
War Diary	Petit Pont Ploegsteert	01/05/1916	31/05/1916
Heading	73rd Machine Gun Company. June 1916		
Miscellaneous	The D.A.G., G.H.Q. 3rd Echelon.		
War Diary	Petit Pont	02/06/1916	17/06/1916
War Diary	Kemmel	19/06/1916	30/06/1916
Heading	73rd Machine Gun Company. July 1916		
War Diary	Kemmel	01/07/1916	19/07/1916
War Diary	Caestre	20/07/1916	25/07/1916
War Diary	Montagne	26/07/1916	31/07/1916
War Diary	Operation Orders.		
Operation(al) Order(s)	73rd. Coy. Machine Gun Corps. Operation Order. No. 1	04/07/1916	04/07/1916
Operation(al) Order(s)	73rd. Coy. Machine Gun Corps. Operation Order. No. 2	06/07/1916	06/07/1916
Operation(al) Order(s)	73rd. Coy. Machine Gun Corps. Operation Order. No. 3	17/07/1916	17/07/1916
Miscellaneous	73 Company, Machine Gun Corps Move Order	23/07/1916	23/07/1916
Heading	73rd Machine Gun Company August 1916		
War Diary	Corbie	01/08/1916	02/08/1916
War Diary	Happy Valley	03/08/1916	08/08/1916
War Diary	Nr Citadel	09/08/1916	16/08/1916
War Diary	Happy Valley	17/08/1916	22/08/1916
War Diary	Sandpit	23/08/1916	25/08/1916
War Diary	Happy Valley	26/08/1916	26/08/1916
War Diary	Buire	27/08/1916	30/08/1916
War Diary	Becordel	31/08/1916	31/08/1916
Miscellaneous	Fighting Order Will Be As Follows	16/08/1916	16/08/1916
Miscellaneous	73 Company Machine Gun Corps. Orders Re Relief. (17/8/16)		
Miscellaneous	73 Company, Machine Gun Corps.	16/08/1916	16/08/1916
Miscellaneous	Position Of Guns	18/08/1916	18/08/1916
Operation(al) Order(s)	73 Coy. M. Gun Corps. O.O. No. 6	30/08/1916	30/08/1916
Heading	73rd Machine Gun Company September 1916		
Miscellaneous		01/10/1916	01/10/1916
War Diary	Becordel	01/09/1916	05/09/1916
War Diary	Dernancourt	06/09/1916	06/09/1916
War Diary	Bauchons	07/09/1916	19/09/1916
War Diary	Marles Ez Mines	20/09/1916	21/09/1916
War Diary	Houdain	22/09/1916	22/09/1916
War Diary	Camblain L'Abbe	23/09/1916	25/09/1916
War Diary	Couy-Servins	26/09/1916	26/09/1916
War Diary	Villers-Au-Bois	27/09/1916	30/09/1916

Miscellaneous	73rd Machine Gun Company October 1916		
Miscellaneous	73 L.B		
War Diary	Villers-Au-Bois	01/10/1916	17/10/1916
War Diary	Camblain L'Abbe	18/10/1916	28/10/1916
War Diary	Mazingarbe	28/10/1916	28/10/1916
War Diary	Les Brebis	31/10/1916	31/10/1916
Operation(al) Order(s)	73rd Company, Machine Gun Corps. Operation Order No. 7	10/10/1916	10/10/1916
Operation(al) Order(s)	73rd Machine Gun Company. Operation Order No. 8	18/10/1916	18/10/1916
Miscellaneous	Time Table Issued With 73rd Machine Gun Company Operation Order No. 8		
Operation(al) Order(s)	73rd Machine Gun Company Operation Order No 9		
Miscellaneous	Relief Orders for Night of October 28/29/16		
Heading	73rd Machine Gun Company. November 1916		
Heading	73rd Machine Gun Company War Diary for month of November 1916		
War Diary	Les Brebis	01/11/1916	30/11/1916
Operation(al) Order(s)	73rd Machine Gun Company Operation Order No. 11	04/11/1916	04/11/1916
Miscellaneous	War Diary		
Operation(al) Order(s)	73rd Machine Gun Company. Operation Order No. 12		
Operation(al) Order(s)	73rd Machine Gun Company. Operation Order No. 13		
Operation(al) Order(s)	73rd Machine Gun Company. Operation Order No. 14		
Miscellaneous	War Diary		
Heading	73rd Machine Gun Company. December 1916		
Heading	War Diary Of 73rd Machine Gun Company for the month of December 1916		
War Diary	Les Brebis	01/12/1916	31/12/1916
Operation(al) Order(s)	73rd Machine Gun Company Operation Order No. 15	03/12/1916	03/12/1916
Miscellaneous	War Diary		
Operation(al) Order(s)	73rd Machine Gun Company. Operation Order No. 16		
Miscellaneous	Positions Of Teams By Sections When Relief Has Been Completed.		
Operation(al) Order(s)	73rd Machine Gun Company Operation Order No. 17	15/12/1916	15/12/1916
Operation(al) Order(s)	73rd Machine Gun Company Operation Order No. 18		
Miscellaneous	War Diary		
Miscellaneous			
Operation(al) Order(s)	73rd Machine Gun Company Operation Order No. 19	27/12/1916	27/12/1916
Miscellaneous	War Diary		
Operation(al) Order(s)	73rd Machine Gun Company Operation Order No. 20	28/12/1916	28/12/1916
Miscellaneous	War Diary		
Heading	War Diary of 73rd Machine Gun Company for the month of January 1917		
War Diary	Les Brebis	01/01/1917	31/01/1917
Operation(al) Order(s)	73rd Machine Gun Company Operation Order No. 21	03/01/1918	03/01/1918
Operation(al) Order(s)	73rd Machine Gun Company Operation Order No. 22	11/01/1917	11/01/1917
Miscellaneous	War Diary		
Operation(al) Order(s)	73rd Machine Gun Company Operation Order No. 25.	24/01/1917	24/01/1917
Operation(al) Order(s)	73rd Machine Gun Company Operation Order No. 23	16/01/1917	16/01/1917
Operation(al) Order(s)	73rd Machine Gun Company Operation Order No. 26	28/01/1917	28/01/1917
Operation(al) Order(s)	73rd Machine Gun Company Amendment to Operation Order No. 26		
Heading	War Diary of 73rd Machine Gun Company For The Month Of February 1917		
War Diary	Les Brebis	01/02/1917	10/02/1917
War Diary	Noeux Les Mines	11/02/1917	11/02/1917
War Diary	Labeuvriere	12/02/1917	28/02/1917

Type	Description	Start	End
Operation(al) Order(s)	73rd Machine Gun Company. Operation Order No 27	04/02/1917	04/02/1917
Operation(al) Order(s)	73rd Machine Gun Company. Operation Order No 28	09/02/1917	09/02/1917
Miscellaneous	73 Coy. Machine Gun Corps. Programme of Work.		
Miscellaneous	73rd. Machine Gun Company. Programme Of Training For Week Ending March 3rd 1917.		
Heading	War Diary For The Month Of March 1917 Of 73rd Machine Gun Company		
War Diary	Labeuvriere	01/03/1917	02/03/1917
War Diary	Haillicourt	03/03/1917	05/03/1917
War Diary	Noulette Wood	06/03/1917	30/03/1917
Operation(al) Order(s)	73 Company Machine Gun Corps. Operation Order No. 29	04/03/1917	04/03/1917
Operation(al) Order(s)	73 Company Machine Gun Corps. Operation Order No. 30	12/03/1917	12/03/1917
Miscellaneous	Appendix A. issued with 73rd Machine Gun Company Operation Order No. 30		
Operation(al) Order(s)	73rd Machine Gun Company. Operation Order No. 31	23/03/1917	23/03/1917
Heading	73rd Brigade Machine Gun Company 24th Division April 1917		
War Diary	Noulette Huts	01/04/1917	20/04/1917
War Diary	Petit Sains	21/04/1917	22/04/1917
War Diary	Marles Les Mines	23/04/1917	23/04/1917
War Diary	Linghem	24/04/1917	26/04/1917
War Diary	Auchel	27/04/1917	27/04/1917
War Diary	Noeux Les Mines	28/04/1917	30/04/1917
Miscellaneous	Brigade Major. 73rd Infantry Brigade.	30/04/1917	30/04/1917
Operation(al) Order(s)	Operation Order. by Major H. Gilbert. M.C. Commanding 73rd Machine Gun Company.	20/04/1917	20/04/1917
Heading	War Diary of 73rd Machine Gun Coy for month of May 1917		
War Diary	Noeux Les Mines	01/05/1917	05/05/1917
War Diary	Labeuvriere	06/05/1917	09/05/1917
War Diary	L'Ecleme	10/05/1917	10/05/1917
War Diary	Thiennes	11/05/1917	12/05/1917
War Diary	Steenvoorde	13/05/1917	14/05/1917
War Diary	Devonshire Camp.	15/05/1917	29/05/1917
War Diary	25 Camp. Zevecoten	30/05/1917	31/05/1917
Heading	73rd Machine Gun Company for the month of June 1917		
War Diary	Zevecoten	01/06/1917	06/06/1917
War Diary	Ouderdom	07/06/1917	13/06/1917
War Diary	Micmac Camp	14/06/1917	27/06/1917
War Diary	Bayenghem	27/06/1917	30/06/1917
Heading	War Diary of 73rd Machine Gun Company for month of July 1917		
War Diary	Bayenghem	01/07/1917	09/07/1917
War Diary	Le Wast	10/07/1917	10/07/1917
War Diary	Bayenghem	11/07/1917	18/07/1917
War Diary	Le Nieppe	19/07/1917	19/07/1917
War Diary	Caestre	20/07/1917	20/07/1917
War Diary	Eeke	21/07/1917	21/07/1917
War Diary	Reninghelst	22/07/1917	22/07/1917
War Diary	Micmac	23/07/1917	31/07/1917
Heading	73rd. Machine Gun Company for the month of August 1917		
War Diary	Micmac Camp	01/08/1917	05/08/1917

War Diary	Micmac	05/08/1917	07/08/1917
War Diary	M Camp Dickebusche	08/08/1917	11/08/1917
War Diary	Line	12/08/1917	17/08/1917
War Diary	Micmac	18/08/1917	19/08/1917
War Diary	M Camp Dickebusch	20/08/1917	20/08/1917
War Diary	Duke Busch	21/08/1917	21/08/1917
War Diary	Line	22/08/1917	27/08/1917
War Diary	Micmac	28/08/1917	30/09/1917
Heading	73rd Machine Gun Company for the month of September 1917		
War Diary	Dickebusche	01/09/1917	03/09/1917
War Diary	Line	04/09/1917	07/09/1917
War Diary	Micmac	08/09/1917	11/09/1917
War Diary	Dickebusche	12/09/1917	14/09/1917
War Diary	Westoutre	15/09/1917	15/09/1917
War Diary	Berquin	16/09/1917	20/09/1917
War Diary	Train	21/09/1917	21/09/1917
War Diary	Barastre	22/09/1917	24/09/1917
War Diary	Haut Allaines	25/09/1917	26/09/1917
War Diary	Line	27/09/1917	30/09/1917
Heading	73rd. Machine Gun Company for the month of October 1917		
War Diary	Line	01/10/1917	14/10/1917
War Diary	Templeux	14/10/1917	31/10/1917
Operation(al) Order(s)	73rd Machine Gun Company. Operation Order By Captain. C.E.R. Croager. M.C. For Relief and change over of positions on the 14th inst.	13/10/1917	13/10/1917
Miscellaneous	Operation Order By Captain. C.E.R. Croager. M.C. For Relief and change over of positions on the 21st inst.	20/10/1917	20/10/1917
Operation(al) Order(s)	Operation Order No. 4 by Captain. C.E.R. Croager M.C. Commanding 73rd Machine Gun Company.	26/10/1917	26/10/1917
Operation(al) Order(s)	Operation Order No.5 by Captain. C.E.R. Croager M.C. Commanding 73rd Machine Gun Company.	28/10/1917	28/10/1917
Heading	73rd Machine Gun Company for the month of November 1917		
War Diary	Templeux-le-Guerard	01/11/1917	11/11/1917
War Diary	Templeux	12/11/1917	18/11/1917
War Diary	Hargicourt	19/11/1917	20/11/1917
War Diary	Templeux	21/11/1917	30/11/1917
Operation(al) Order(s)	Operation Order No. 7. by Captain. C.E.R. Croager. M.C. Commanding 73rd Machine Gun Company.	08/11/1917	08/11/1917
Operation(al) Order(s)	Operation Order No. 8 by Lieutenant. P.M. Andrews. Commanding 73rd Machine Gun Company.	14/11/1917	14/11/1917
Operation(al) Order(s)	Operation Order No. 9 by Lieutenant. P.M. Andrews. Commanding 73rd Machine Gun Company.	21/11/1917	21/11/1917
Miscellaneous	Operation Order No. 10 by Lieutenant. P.M. Andrews. Commanding 73rd Machine Gun Company.	27/11/1917	27/11/1917
Heading	73rd Machine Gun Company for the month of December 1917		
War Diary	Templeux	01/12/1917	18/12/1917
War Diary	Hervilly	19/12/1917	26/12/1917
War Diary	Templeux	27/12/1917	31/12/1917
Heading	73rd Machine Gun Company for the month of January 1918		
War Diary	Templeux	01/01/1918	04/01/1918
War Diary	Hervilly	05/01/1918	07/01/1918

War Diary	Vraignes	08/01/1918	19/01/1918
War Diary	Hargicourt	20/01/1918	28/01/1918
War Diary	Hervilly	29/01/1918	31/01/1918
Heading	73rd Machine Gun Company for the month of February 1918		
War Diary	Hervilly	01/02/1918	15/02/1918
War Diary	Hargicourt	16/02/1918	22/02/1918
War Diary	Templeux Quarry	23/02/1918	28/02/1918

WO 95
2219/3

24TH DIVISION
73RD INFY BDE

73RD MACHINE GUN COY
FEB 1916-FEB 1918

24TH DIVISION
73RD INFY BDE

73rd Brigade.
24th Division.

Disembarked HAVRE from U.K. 11.3.16.

73rd MACHINE GUN COMPANY.

22nd FEBRUARY to 31st MAY

1 9 1 6

Feb '18

73rd Brigade.
24th Division.

Disembarked HAVRE from U.K. 11.3.16.

73rd MACHINE GUN COMPANY.

2nd FEBRUARY TO 1st MAY 1916.

The D.A.G.,

    3rd Echelon,

        The Base.

        Herewith Army Form C.2118 (War Diary) for the Company under my command from 22/2/16 to 1st May, 1916.

In the field.   *signature* Captain,

4/5/16.   Commanding 73rd Brigade Machine Gun Company.

Army Form C. 2118.

WAR DIARY
or
INTELLIGENCE SUMMARY.
(Erase heading not required.)

Instructions regarding War Diaries and Intelligence Summaries are contained in F. S. Regs., Part II. and the Staff Manual respectively. Title pages will be prepared in manuscript.

Place	Date	Hour	Summary of Events and Information	Remarks and references to Appendices
(OUDERDOM)	22/2/16		First day of Mobilisation.	WG
—	10/3/16		Left GRANTHAM and entrained at SOUTHAMPTON at. Transport Tman body in separate boats	WG
—	11/3/16		Disembarked HAVRE and proceeded to No.1. Details Rest Camp.	WG
—			1 O.R. admitted hospital.	WG
—	12/3/16		Encamped HAVRE.	WG
—	13/3/16		Entrained at GARE MARITIME Pt 6. 12.30 a.m.	WG
—			Detrained POPERINGHE 11 p.m. and encamped at place Map reference Sheet 28 (YPRES) H.13.c.7.3	WG
—	15/3/16		The Coy was inspected by MAJOR GEN. J.E. CAPPER. C.B Comm.g. 24th Div. at 10 a.m.	WG
—	17/3/16		1 Mule destroyed, 1 O.R. admitted hospital.	WG
—	18/3/16		Left POPERINGHE and marched in Brigade column to billets near METEREN (Sheet 27, X.1.d.2.2.)	WG
—			2nd LIEUT. G.G. RAMAGE admitted hospital.	WG
—	19/3/16		1 O.R. admitted hospital, 1 O.R. discharged hospital.	WG
—	20/3/16		1 O.R. admitted hospital.	WG
—	21/3/16		1 O.R. admitted hospital	WG
—	22/3/16		2 O.R. admitted hospital.	WG
—	23/3/16		No 1 & 2 Sections under O.C. Coy left METEREN and marched to COURT DREVE (Sheet 28 T.24.a.9.6)	WG

Army Form C. 2118.

WAR DIARY
or
INTELLIGENCE SUMMARY.
(Erase heading not required.)

Instructions regarding War Diaries and Intelligence Summaries are contained in F. S. Regs., Part II. and the Staff Manual respectively. Title pages will be prepared in manuscript.

Place	Date	Hour	Summary of Events and Information	Remarks and references to Appendices
COURT DREVE (Sh.28. T29a.4.6)	29/3/16		The 6 guns of these sections took over (same night) firing positions from Mach Gun Coy of 3rd Canadian Inf Bde.	MG
			Remainder of Coy (3 + 4 sections and HdQrs under 2nd Lieut. T.H.D. BELL left METEREN and marched to COURT DREVE (Coy. Billet) evacuated by 3rd CANADIAN INF BDE M.G. Coy same day.	MG
—	28/3/16		1. O.R. discharged hospital.	MG
—	29/3/16		The following details attached to Company.	
			9th Royal Sussex Regt. — 6. O.R.	
			7th. Northampton Regt. — 10. O.R.	
			13th. Middlesex Regt. — 6. O.R.	
—	30/3/16		1. O.R. wounded in action.	MG
—	2/4/16		2nd LIEUT. T.H.D. BELL (accompanied by 1 O.R.) proceeded to Adv. M.T. Depot. ABBEVILLE for a course of transport duties.	MG
—	4/4/16		2. O.R. reinforcements joined from Base. 1. O.R. discharged hospital.	MG
—	5/4/16		1, O.R. admitted hospital. 1. O.R. wounded in action.	MG
—	6/4/16		Coy. moved into new billet at PETIT PONT, (T.2.3.6.2.2. Sheet 28) until this date occupied by 17th Bde. Machine Gun Coy.	MG

Army Form C. 2118.

WAR DIARY
or
INTELLIGENCE SUMMARY.
(Erase heading not required.)

Instructions regarding War Diaries and Intelligence Summaries are contained in F. S. Regs., Part II. and the Staff Manual respectively. Title pages will be prepared in manuscript.

Place	Date	Hour	Summary of Events and Information	Remarks and references to Appendices
PETIT PONT Slip de Faubert	8/4/16		6 O.R. reinforcements joined from Base.	MG
-	11/4/16		1 O.R. (wounded) discharged hospital to duty.	MG
-	15/4/16		2/Lt. W J GURNEY wounded in action (G.S.W. back)	MG
-	17/4/16		3 O.R. admitted to hospital.	MG
-	18/4/16		2/Lt. P. POUNTNEY joined as reinforcement.	
			Mobilization table (New edition) allows for an extra officer, and one man.	MG
-	19/4/16		2 O.R. joined as reinforcement.	MG
-	25/4/16		2/Lt. T.H.D. BELL returned from transport convoy.	MG
-	29/4/16		About 1 am Klaxon horns gave warning of gas. 1 Coll Shoer attached to Coy. The Coy 'stood to' but on no message being received from Bde HdQrs stood down about 2 am. It was an entirely false alarm as far as our Bde front was concerned.	
			12 midnight a message was received via Bde HdQrs (from 72nd Bde (on our left) that a gas attack was immediately imminent.	MG
-	30/4/16		12.45. am Gas was released from German front line/personally seen by O.C. Coy.)	
			1 am. "TAKE ACTION" received from Bde. Message transmitted to transport-limber. All reserve guns were in position by 3.10. am. During the passage of the gas all guns fired	

T2134. Wt. W708-776. 500000. 4/15. Sir J. C. & S.

Army Form C. 2118.

WAR DIARY
or
INTELLIGENCE SUMMARY.
(Erase heading not required.)

Instructions regarding War Diaries and Intelligence
Summaries are contained in F.S. Regs., Part II.
and the Staff Manual respectively. Title pages
will be prepared in manuscript.

Place	Date	Hour	Summary of Events and Information	Remarks and references to Appendices
PETIT POTT	30/4/16	11 p.m.	Fragment bursts and suffered no deleterious effect. There was no infantry attack. 'Stand down' was ordered at about 5 a.m., and normal routine resumed.	MG
—	1/5/16	12.30 a.m.	Bombardment heard & Coy 'stood to'. 'Stand down' ordered by Bde.	MG
—			'Stand to' ordered by Bde at 11.10 p.m.	MG

W. Sidell.
—————— CAPTAIN,
COMMANDING No. 73 M. G. COY.,
MACHINE GUN CORPS.

The D.A.G,

    3rd Echelon, The Base

    Herewith original War Diary for the month of May, 1916, for the company under my command.

In the field.   Captain,
31/5/16.   Commanding 73rd Brigade Machine Gun Company.

73. M.G. Coy 1
Army Form C. 2118.
Vol 2

WAR DIARY
or
INTELLIGENCE SUMMARY.
(Erase heading not required.)

Instructions regarding War Diaries and Intelligence Summaries are contained in F.S. Regs., Part II. and the Staff Manual respectively. Title pages will be prepared in manuscript.

Place	Date	Hour	Summary of Events and Information	Remarks and references to Appendices
PETIT PONT — PLOEG-STEERT	MAY 1	2.30 pm	2 O.R. wounded in action	
			Water cart to Army Ordnance Dept. for overhaul, petrol cans being used for drawing & storage of water	
	2		1 O.R. admitted — 1 O.R. discharged Hospital to duty.	
	3	1.50 pm	2 L. G.R. ANDERSON joined (reinforcement) from Base.	
	4	2.30 pm	1 O.R. joined (re-inforcement) from Base.	
			1 O.R. to Hospital	
	5		Water cart returned from A.O.D. completed.	
	7		8 O.R. proceeded to M.G. Corps Base Depot CAMIERS for further instruction in Machine Guns. (Shown if strength of Company. Authority A-2130 24th Divn.)	
			4 O.R. transferred from 9th R. SUSSEX to O.R. from 7 NORTHAMPTONS to replace above. These are taken from those attached to Coy from 29th March 1916.	
			MAJOR LINDSAY of the M.G.T.C. Staff made a tour of inspection of the Coys position in the line	

WAR DIARY or INTELLIGENCE SUMMARY

Army Form C. 2118.

Place	Date	Hour	Summary of Events and Information	Remarks and references to Appendices
PETIT PONT – PLOEG-STEERT	MAY 7 (cont)	8:30 pm	2 Lt. H.A. WOOD late XI th GORDONS arrived as reinforcement from Base	MW
	9		1 OR admitted to Hospital	
	10		1 OR admitted to Hospital	
	11		2 OR proceeded to Bailleul for Course of Signalling.	
	13		2 OR admitted to Hospital.	
	16		1 OR discharged Hospital	
	17		1 OR discharged Hospital.	
	18	12:30 am	Gas alarm sounded in Thombu Hem in Billet, apparently taken up from some distance away south. Here was in fact a bombardment on our front. The Company stood to until 1:0 AM when Brigade sent order to stand down.	
			Notification by 36th M.V.S. of the evacuation of 1 Mule on 8 MAY. Disease Arthritis.	MW

Army Form C. 2118.

WAR DIARY
or
INTELLIGENCE SUMMARY.
(Erase heading not required.)

Instructions regarding War Diaries and Intelligence Summaries are contained in F.S. Regs., Part II. and the Staff Manual respectively. Title pages will be prepared in manuscript.

Place	Date	Hour	Summary of Events and Information	Remarks and references to Appendices
PETIT POM PLOEG STEERT	19		1OR rejoined Company from M.G. School Camiers.	
			1OR granted leave with Ration Allowance from 17th to 25th May 1916	
	21		2Lt. G.R.ANDERSON & 2OR proceeded from BAILLEUL to CAMIERS for Course of Instruction at M.G. School.	
			1OR granted leave with Ration Allowance from 21 May to 29 May.	
	21		2OR arrived as reinforcement from Base.	
	25		1OR admitted to Hospital.	
	27		2OR arrived as reinforcements from Base	
	29		1OR wounded in action.	
			1OR proceeded to UK today to take up employment as a munition worker (Nutting A+1 OMG 24th DIV. A/3969/M.F. 27.5.16 CR No. 25300/25 & 73rd I.B. No. DC. 771. 27/5/16.)	
	30		1OR proceeded on leave with Ration allowance from 30 May to 6 June.	
	31		1OR proceeded to No 22 Vety Hospital ABBEVILLE for a Course of Farriery.	MW

73rd Brigade.
24th Division.

73rd MACHINE GUN COMPANY.

JUNE 1916.

The D.A.G.,

    G.H.Q.,

        3rd Echelon.

Herewith the original copy of the War Diary

of 3 company M.G. corps for the month of June

1918.

-------- Captain,

Commanding No. 73 M.G. Coy.,

Machine Gun Corps.

73 M.G. Coy
Army Form C. 2118.
Vol 3
June
XXIV

WAR DIARY or INTELLIGENCE SUMMARY.

Place	Date	Hour	Summary of Events and Information	Remarks and references to Appendices
PETIT PORT	2		2 O.R wounded in action 1 of which died of wounds.	MD
	3		1 O.R to Hospital	MD
	4		2 O.R attached - returned to their own units & were replaced by 2 O.R from same units	
	8		1 O.R discharged hospital	MD
			1 O.R leave to U.K.	MD
			1 O.R leave to U.K.	MD
	10		2/Lt TH.D.BELL leave to U.K.	MD
	9		1 O.R discharged hospital	MD
	14		1 O.R leave to U.K.	MD
	15		1 O.R discharged hospital	MD
			1 O.R admitted hospital	MD
	15		2/Lt L.B. MAUNSELL & 5 O.R joined from Base	MD
	16		2 O.R admitted to hospital	MD
	17	1.30 am	Hostile gas attack on our front. 9 O.R wounded (of which 5 now gassed) All admitted hospital.	MD

Army Form C. 2118.

WAR DIARY
or
INTELLIGENCE SUMMARY.
(Erase heading not required.)

Instructions regarding War Diaries and Intelligence Summaries are contained in F. S. Regs., Part II. and the Staff Manual respectively. Title pages will be prepared in manuscript.

Place	Date	Hour	Summary of Events and Information	Remarks and references to Appendices
PETIT PONT	17	9 am	Billet shelled till noon. Company & horses scattered in fields. Horses in rear of billet. No casualties from this bombardment.	MM
		2 pm	Moved by march route to camp at Kemmel Hill. Took over camp from 150th M.G. Coy.	MM
	18		being relieved at PETIT PONT by 7th Australian Bde M.G. Coy who took over our sector in line.	MM
KEMMEL	19		2 OR admitted Hospital.	MM
	22		2 OR admitted Hospital.	MM
	27		1 OR leave to U.K. 1 OR discharged Hospital.	MM
	28		1 horse (light draught) died Septic poisoning from deep wound in near hind. 2 OR from Base reinforcements.	MM
	25		Reinforcement 2 Mules.	MM
	29		1 OR admitted Hospital.	MM
	30.		2 OR discharged Hospital.	MM

J. ? Capt
Cmndg ? M.G. ?

73rd Inf.Bde.
24th Div.

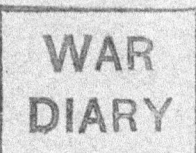

73rd MACHINE GUN COMPANY.

J U L Y

1 9 1 6

Attached:

Operation Orders.

WAR DIARY
or
INTELLIGENCE SUMMARY.

Army Form C. 2118.

(Erase heading not required.)

Place	Date	Hour	Summary of Events and Information	Remarks and references to Appendices
KEMMEL	Feb 1		1 O.R. to 22 Vet Hospital ABBEVILLE for course of cold shoeing	F.D.L.
			1 O.R. returned to duty from course of Machine Gunnery. M.Gun Sch. CAMMIERS.	F.D.L.
	2		1 O.R. discharged Hospital. 1 O.R. admitted Hospital.	F.D.L.
	3		2 O.R. to M. Gun Sch. CAMIERS for course of instruction.	
			1 O.R. admitted to Hospital	
			6 guns relieved by 14th M.G. Coy	F.D.L.
	4		1 O.R. to U.K. for work as known letter Auth. W.O. 19/released/4110 (A.G.5) dated	F.D.L.
			1/5/16. 1 O.R. discharged Hospital.	F.D.L.
	5		10 O.R. joined from base as reinforcements	F.D.L.
			Relief carried out in line as per O.O. No 1. (attached)	F.D.L.
	6		1 O.R. Wounded in action.	F.D.L.
	7		Transport lines moved to LOCRE owing to proximity of artillery.	F.D.L.
			Relief carried out in line as per O.O. No 2 (attached)	
	8		Coy relieved in trenches by 150th K.G. Coy.	F.D.L.
	9		1 O.R. from course of signalling at 2nd Div. Sig Sch.	F.D.L.
	11		Coy moved to SPIERSTRAAT near NEUVE ÉGLISE.	F.D.L.

WAR DIARY or INTELLIGENCE SUMMARY.

Army Form C. 2118.

Place	Date	Hour	Summary of Events and Information	Remarks and references to Appendices
KEMMEL	11.		Took over 4 gun positions from 17th M.G. Coy & 2 gun positions from 2nd Northampton Regt.	EDL
	13.		Took over 4 manned 1 gun position from same gunners of Northampton Regt.	EDL
	14.		1.O.R. to M.G.C. Base Depot as inefficient.	EDL
	15.		1.O.R. admitted Hospital. 2.O.R. attached from Regts. in Brigade returning to their Units as unsuitable for M.G. work. Notification from G.H.Q. of final transfer of 9 O.R. from Regts. in Brigade.	EDL
	16.		1.O.R. admitted Hospital.	EDL
	17.		1 O.R. do do	EDL
	18.		2.O.R. (reinforcements) joined from Base.	EDL
	19.		Relief in trenches by 61st A.G. Coy vide O.O. No 3 attached.	EDL
	18.		Relief carried out in trenches vide O.O. No 3.	EDL
	19.		Relieved in line by 61st Coy M.G.C.	EDL
CAESTRE.	20.		1 O.R. discharged Hospital.	EDL
	21.		2.O.R. returned from M.G. course to un Units at CAESTRE. Coy moved to M.G. School CAMIERS.	EDL
	22.		3.O.R. admitted Hospital.	EDL
	22.		1.O.R. returned to duty from attached to 24th Div. train as temp. unfit.	EDL
	"		2/Lt. P. POUNTNEY to 19th Coy M.G.C. Auth. A.G.A.M. 18 dated 20/7/16.	EDL

WAR DIARY
or
INTELLIGENCE SUMMARY.
(Erase heading not required.)

Army Form 2118.

Place	Date	Hour	Summary of Events and Information	Remarks and references to Appendices
CAESTRE	22		2 O.R. from H.G. Course H.G. School CAMIERS.	KOT
	23		7 O.R. to Base Depot of H.G.C. as inefficient. Application for transfer of 6 O.R. from attached to partly replace. 1 Sergt. from Base Depot as reinforcement. 2 O.R. to Hospital.	EO
	25		Entrained at GODEWAERSVELDE at 11.40 a.m. Arrived at SALEUX at 9 p.m. Marched with transport to MONTAGNE - (SOMME) & billetted there. Vide Move Order E.O.	EO
MONTAGNE	26		640 R. (16 from each Bn in Brigade) sent for 5 hours training daily in Amm. Carrying duties with the Cavy, with a view to using them for this duty in action. 1 O.R. to Hospital.	EO
	28		1 O.R. reinforcement from Base.	EO
	29		1 O.R. from Course of Colt Shoeing at No 1 ABBEVILLE. 1 O.R. from Hospital. Transport under 2/Lt J.H. Bell left at 1 p.m. to proceed by road with Brigade transport to VECQUEMONT.	EO
	30			EO
	31.		Coy. paraded at 3 a.m. marched to HANGEST where they entrained. Detrained at VECQUEMONT at 12.30. Marched to billets in CORBIE. arriving 5.45 p.m. Transport under 2/Lt J.H. Bell arrived 4.50 p.m.	EO

Bishop Capt
Commg 73 M.G. Coy.

OPERATION ORDERS.

Ref. Trench map   73rd. Coy. MACHINE GUN CORPS.   Copy No. 2
MESSINES 1/10,000.
                O P E R A T I O N   O R D E R.   N O. 1.   4/7/16.

1. The following reliefs will be carried out during the afternoon and night of July 5/6th.
      No.1. Section. (a) Will relieve SPY FARM.
                    (b) Will relieve No.2. Section in S.P.10.

      No.2. Section. (a) Will relieve No. 3. Section in VIA GELLIA.
                    (b) Will relieve No. 3. Section in FORT REGINA.

      No.3. Section. (a) Will relieve No. 4. Section in H4.
                    (b) Will relieve No. 4. Section in S.P.11.
                    (c) Will relieve POLKA FARM.

      No.4. Section. (a) Will relieve No. 3. Section (1 gun) in POLKA FARM.
                    (b) Will relieve S.P.11a.

2. The following can be relieved during the afternoon:-
       SPY FARM, POLKA FARM (1 gun No. 3. Section).

3. All teams, with the exception of H4., will go to their new positions during the afternoon, and dump their equipment. N.C.Os. will thoroughly reconnoitre their positions by daylight.

4. Teams will meet their limbers at the following places:-
         S.P.10.   PARRAIN FARM.
         VIA GELLIA.   PARRAIN FARM.
         FORT REGINA   N 22 c 7½. 2.
         S.P.11.   PARRAIN FARM.
         POLKA FARM.   POLKA FARM.
No.1. Section will require one limber to PARRAIN FARM for S.P.10.
No.2. Section will require one limber for FORT REGINA & PARRAIN FARM
        (for VIA GELLIA) & to bring out gun from S.P.10.
No.3. Section will require one limber to ROSSIGNOL DUMP for H4. & to
        bring out No.4. Section gun.
           Also one limber to PARRAIN FARM for S.P.11. & to bring
        out gun from FORT REGINA.
No.4. Section will require one limber to POLKA FARM with one gun & then
        on to PARRAIN FARM to bring out gun from VIA GELLIA.

5. All rations for the 6th will be carried up by the teams.

6. Future ration arrangements:-
      Right Sector Limber. SPY FARM, FORT REGINA, S.Ps. 10, 11, 11a, VIA
                       SPY FARM get rations from REGINA.   GELLIA.
      Left Sector Limber. POLKA FARM, S.P.12., H4.
                       H4. rations will be sent up to them.

7. Section Officers will send in by returning teams notes reporting their own section reliefs complete.

8. Equipment returns will be taken in by Section Officers and personally completed for each of their positions, and returned to H.Q. by night 8/9th

9. Section Officers will live at the following places:-
         No.1. Section.   S.P.10.
         No.2.   :   POLKA FARM.
         No.3.   :   :   :
         No.4.   :   S.P.12.

10. Supervision of teams will be made easier under arrangements between Section Officers direct, by arranging that:-
No.4. S.O. supervises H4.   No.3. Section Off. supervises POLKA FARM.

11. All other details between O.C's. Sections direct.

12. All copies except Nos. 1 & 2 will be destroyed when relief is complete.

                                                     Capt.
                                Commdg. 73rd. Coy. M.G.C.
                                                                P.T.O.

COPY NO. 1. File.
2. War Diary.
3. O.C.
4. Lt. Springfield.
5. 2/Lt. Bleck.
6.   Dove.
7.   Wood.
8.   Anderson.
9.   Tibbitt.
10.   Maunsell.
11.   Pountney.
12. Transport Officer.
13. S.M.
14. Q.M.S.
15. Sergt. Hubbard.
16.   :   Todd.

Ref. Trench Map   73 Company, Machine Gun Corps.   Copy No. 2
MESSINES 1/10,000.

OPERATION ORDER NO. 2   6/7/16.

1. No. 3 Section complete will be withdrawn from the line during night of July 7th/8th.

2. The following reliefs will be carried out on the night of July 7th/8th.

    No. 1 Section will relieve No. 3 Section in FORT REGINA.

    No. 2 Section will relieve No. 3 Section in POLKA FARM
    No. 2 Section will relieve No. 3 Section in S.P.11.
    No. 2 Section will relieve No. 4 Section in S.P.11.a.

    No. 4 Section will relieve No. 3 Section in H.4.

3. All teams, with the exception of H.4., will go to their new positions during the afternoon, and dump their equipment, etc. N.C.O's will thoroughly reconnoitre their positions by daylight.

4. Ration limbers will go up as usual, but Teams can take up their own rations if more convenient.

5. Section Officers will send in by returning Teams notes reporting their own Section reliefs complete.

6. 2nd Lieut Tibbitt will arrange that orderlies leave POLKA FARM at 12 noon for Headquarters, returning to POLKA FARM at 4 p.m. 7/7/16.

7. All other details between O.C's Sections direct also between O.C's and Transport Officer.

8. All copies except Nos 1 & 2 will be destroyed when relief is complete.

Issued at 8 p.m.

                       E.O. Springfield
                             for.   Captain,
    Commanding 73rd Brigade Machine Gun Company.

        Copy No. 1. File.
              2. War Diary.
              3. C.O.
              4. Lt Springfield.
              5. 2/Lt Bleck.
              6.   "   Wood.
              7.   "   Anderson.
              8.   "   Tibbitt.
              9.   "   Dove.
             10.   "   Maunsell.
             11.   "   Pountney.
             12. Transport Officer.
             13. C.S.M.
             14. C.Q.M.S.
             15. Sergt Hubbard.

Ref. Trench Map   73 Company, Machine Gun Corps.   Copy No. 7
MESSINES. 1:10,000.

OPERATION ORDER NO. 3.   17/7/16.

1. The following reliefs will be carried out on the night of July 18/19th.
   No. 1 Section will carry out its own relief.
   No. 2 Section will relieve No. 4 Section complete.
2. Teams will leave camp at 9-15 p.m. They will carry in their own rations for the 19th instant.
3. No. 2 Section will detail 2 men to live at SOUVENIR FARM, to act as orderlies and ration party for the DIAGONAL.
4. No equipment will be handed over between sections. Teams relieved will hand in to Headquarters lists of trench stores taken over by incoming teams.
5. Section Officers will send in by returning teams notes reporting their own section reliefs complete.
6. All other details between O.C. Sections direct, also between O's.C Sections and Transport Officer.
7. All copies except Nos. 1 & 2 will be destroyed when relief is complete.

Issued at. 6.15. p.m.

                               W. Gilbert
                                     Captain,

Commanding 73 Company, Machine Gun Corps.

No. 1 Copy	.... File.	No. 9 Copy	.... 2nd Lieut Dove.
No. 2	" .... War Diary.	No. 10 "	.... " Maunsell.
No. 3	" .... C.O.	No. 11 "	.... " Springfield.
No. 4	" .... 2/Lt Bleck.	No. 12 "	.... " Anderson.
No. 5	" .... " Wood.	No. 13 "	.... " Pountney.
No. 6	" .... C.S.M.	No. 14 "	.... " Tibbitt.
No. 7	" .... C.Q.M.S.	No. 15. "	.... Sergt Hubbard.
No. 8	" .... T.O.		

-:MINOR ENTERPRISE:-

to be carried out tonight by 17th Inf. Bgde. against SPANBROEKMOLEN.

Gas will be discharged on whole of 24th Divisional front at +2 min.
Teams at SHELL FARM and DIAGONAL will wear smoke helmets from Zero time to +15 or longer if necessary.
"Gas Alert" as usual for other teams.
Smoke will be discharged at +2 min., and at +1Hr. 20 min.
Teams will be disposed so as to ensure maximum safety compatible with readiness to act as per defence scheme. THIS ORDER WILL BE STRICTLY OBEYED BY ALL RANKS.
There will be no working parties tonight.
At +1hr. 45 min, artillery cease, except for such counter battery work as may still be required.
No. orders have been received re machine guns. Guns at FORT PINKIE only may be fired at discretion of O.C. No. 1 Section between
+2 min. to +30 min, and
+1 hr. to +1 hr. 45 min.
Fire to be directed opposite our Brigade front only.
This might be a good opportunity of testing guns and newly water-proofed belts.
At +1 hr. 20 min our troops in trenches will cheer.
Zero time is... 11. P.M. ....
Standard time by watch per..... ORDERLY ....

                               W. Gilbert
                                  Captain,

Commanding 73 Company, Machine Gun Corps.

73 Company, Machine Gun Corps.   ~~Copy No.~~

~~OPERATION~~ MOVE ORDER ~~No.~~ 4. 25/7/16.
======================================

1. Reveille tomorrow will be at 4 a.m.
   Breakfast 4-30 a.m.
   All transport vehicles will be packed by 6-30 a.m.
   Parade 7 a.m. near transport lines. Dress full marching order
   Waterbottles filled.

2. Waterbottles will be filled from pump under section arrangements
   Before moving off, the water cart will be filled from the pump.

3. March Discipline.
   ===============   Officers and N.C.Os will see that march
   discipline is strictly enforced.
   No drinking from water bottles will be allowed without permissio

4. Entrainment.
   ===========   Equipment will not be taken off unless ordered,
   and will only be dumped by order of an officer, who is responsible for its dumping in an orderly and satisfactory manner.
   There will be no riding on top or side of carriages. No one will
   get out at stops without permission.

5. Wagons.
   ======   No article of equipment will be left on outside of
   wagons. Special precautions must be taken so that everything
   is securely tied down.

6. Transport.
   =========   Transport will be ready for inspection at 6-50 a.m.
   Pack-saddlery will be carried in the wagons.

7. Inspection of billets.
   ===================   At 6-30 a.m. Section Sergts will report
   condition of billet to section officers, who will make an i
   inspection.

73rd Brigade.
24th Division.

73rd MACHINE GUN COMPANY

AUGUST 1916

VOL 5 "74
Army Form C. 2118.
73 M G C

WAR DIARY
or
INTELLIGENCE SUMMARY.
(Erase heading not required.)

Instructions regarding War Diaries and Intelligence Summaries are contained in F. S. Regs., Part II. and the Staff Manual respectively. Title pages will be prepared in manuscript.

Place	Date	Hour	Summary of Events and Information	Remarks and references to Appendices
CORBIE	Aug 1.		No training parade held. Kit & foot Inspection. Preliminary move order rec'd from Base at 5 p.m. O.O. rec'd at 6 p.m. 3 O.R. as reinforcements from Base	RD
	2.		Following instructions contained in O.O. Coy paraded at 5 A.M. and marched with Sussex & Middlesex to SAILLEY-LE-SEC. Arriving at 6-45 A.M. & bivouaced. Coy bathed in the Canal during the day. Paraded at 6 p.m. & marched with Brigade to HAPPY VALLEY arriving at 9.30 p.m. & bivouaced	RD
HAPPY VALLEY	3		Two hours training. No other parade.	RD
	4.		ditto	RD
	5.	5 p.m.	Two hours training chiefly in the duties of the M.G. teams in the assault. Lecture by Maj. Gen. CAPPER C.B. on duties of all ranks in the assault. Special points brought out.	
			(1) Necessity of setting to work immediately sending back information as regards position	
			(2) " " pushing out outposts while line is being consolidated.	
			(3) " " saving S.A.A. & Water	
			(4) " " gaining ground at this stage of operations	RD

T2131. Wt. W703—776. 500000. 4/15. Sir J. C. & S.

Army Form C. 2118.

WAR DIARY
or
INTELLIGENCE SUMMARY.
(Erase heading not required.)

Instructions regarding War Diaries and Intelligence Summaries are contained in F.S. Regs., Part II. and the Staff Manual respectively. Title pages will be prepared in manuscript.

Place	Date	Hour	Summary of Events and Information	Remarks and references to Appendices
HAPPY VALLEY	6.		96 O.R. (24 from each Batn. in Bde) attacked to the Coy as carried. Accomodation provided by Coy, to be returned by Coy from 9th inst.	R.O.
	7.		4 Officers (1 from each Batn. in Bde) attended for course of training in M.G. work.	
		3 PM	Practised Attack. (1) Very short notice given. (2) Two batts. in attack, frontage about 500ˣ. (3) Objective two lines supposed German trenches about 250ˣ apart. (4) Batn. followed barrage in two waves. (5) Disposition of guns:- 2 guns with 1st batt. in 2nd wave. 2 " " " " " " " 4 guns in reserve.	
	8.		1 O.R. attd. from 1st Northants Regt. returned to his Regt. 10 O.R. to No. G.C. Base Depot under age. Auth. A.C. Instruction No.1186 of 1916. C.R. No. 5544/4252 A. A. & Q.M.G. 24th Div. A/4624/37 of 6-8-16.	R.O.
		12 Noon	Order recd. from Brigade that the Coy would move to new Camp at CITADEL	

WAR DIARY
or
INTELLIGENCE SUMMARY.
(Erase heading not required.)

Army Form C. 2118.

Place	Date	Hour	Summary of Events and Information	Remarks and references to Appendices
Nr. CITADEL		at 3 p.m.	2.O.O.R. under 2Lt / DOVE went forward at 1 p.m. Nos 1 & 2 Sections under Lt E.O. Springfield left HAPPY VALLEY at 3 p.m. Nos 3 & 4 Sections marched independently under Section Officers. All fighting Mules & 2 A.M.M. Limbers accompanied the Coy. Remaining A.M.M. Limbers & all Mules & Horses moved at old transport lines in HAPPY VALLEY under 2Lt Bell. Coy Camp in HAPPY VALLEY handed over to 6th M.G.Coy. Weather, very hot.	E.O.S
	9.	9 AM	Preliminary warning recd. from Brigade at 9 A.M. to hold ourselves in readiness to take over from a Bde. of the 55th Div. C.O.s to reconnoitre line	
		1.30 P.M.	Order cancelled at 1-30 p.m.	
		6.0 P.M.	Definite orders from Bde. that the Coy would not move from the Area the following day (10/7/18) & that training was to be continued. One section (No 3) detailed to parade at 5 A.M. to report at H.Q. 1st NN for training with that Batn. Weather, very hot.	R.O.L
	10	5 A.M	Operations by 1st NN Regt cancelled. No training parades owing to rain. Kit & gun inspections.	Ap

WAR DIARY or INTELLIGENCE SUMMARY.

Army Form C. 2118.

Place	Date	Hour	Summary of Events and Information	Remarks and references to Appendices
Nr. CITADEL	11.		7 O.R. reinforcements from Base Depot. Nos 1 & 2 Sections paraded with 13th Middx Regt & 7th N.N Regt respectively for practice attack. Nos 3 & 4 Sections practised digging in & consolidating. Weather fine.	ETD
	12.		All sections paraded with Lewis guns & equipment & practised consolidation of a bit of old trenches.	ETD
			Lecture by C.O. to Officers & N.C.Os. Subjects Operation Orders & Reports. Preliminary warning received that the 24th Divn had been selected to take the village of GUILLEMONT.	
	13.		3 O.R. reinforcements from Base Depot. Weather cooler some rain. Two hours tactical training in morning, including Gas Drill of all new men. Paraded at 8·30 P.M. continued consolidating in trenches, combining use of Signal Pistols against bombing parties. 2 LT. F.A. PHILPOTT 9th K. Yorks joined as reinforcement.	ETD
	14.		No 1 Section under 2 LT BLECK paraded with 13th Middx Regt for practice attack. Weather cool	ETD

Army Form C. 2118.

WAR DIARY
or
INTELLIGENCE SUMMARY.
(Erase heading not required.)

Instructions regarding War Diaries and Intelligence Summaries are contained in F. S. Regs., Part II. and the Staff Manual respectively. Title pages will be prepared in manuscript.

Place	Date	Hour	Summary of Events and Information	Remarks and references to Appendices
N° CITADEL				
	15.		Nos 2 & 4 Sections four hours training including use of & ammoning & detonating discs for trench fire.	E.O.
			No 1 Section training in use of training discs. Nos 2, 3 & 4 sections further instruction in construction of shell pits etc.	E.O.
	16.		Operation Order No 59 (/3 I.B.) rec. Containing following information. The 24th Div. has been selected to take GUILLEMONT & establish itself on a line on the East & North East of the Village. Final objective for /3 I.B. West edge of GUILLEMONT village from T 25 6 2 5 – 22 4 a 2 5 (Ref. Map. LONGUEVAL 1/10,000) The attack of the /2nd I.B. will be delivered on a frontage of three battalions, two Coys in support & two in Brigade Reserve. ACTION FOR MACHINE GUNS. First line of 6 our guns, two with each Batt., to go forward with the 2nd wave. Second line of our guns to remain stationary during attack & give covering fire.	

Army Form C. 2118.

WAR DIARY
or
INTELLIGENCE SUMMARY.
(Erase heading not required.)

Instructions regarding War Diaries and Intelligence Summaries are contained in F.S. Regs., Part II. and the Staff Manual respectively. Title pages will be prepared in manuscript.

Place	Date	Hour	Summary of Events and Information	Remarks and references to Appendices
Nr. CITADEL			Reserve of four guns in vicinity of Battle Headquarters. 151 B.OO No 60 recd. ordering two guns to report to O.C. 2nd Knights Regt. & Lt. BLECK with two teams of No 1 Sect. detailed. Remainder of Coy ordered to relieve Y2 M.G. Coy in the line. Non-combatant portion of Coy including recent reinforcements moved to Transport Rinic in HAPPY VALLEY	K.O.R.
		11.15pm	Above relief cancelled.	
HAPPY VALLEY	14.		1 O.R. admitted hospital. Orders received that Y3rd I.B. would relieve Y2nd I.B. in the line during daylight. We to keep fighting orders as detailed or attached. Orders re relief as per attached. Relief greatly hindered by heavy enemy shelling but completed by 6 AM 15/7/16. Casualties: M.G.C. 1 O.R. wounded. Attached from Y 4th Northamptonshires 1 O.R. wounded. Coy Hd Qrs established S.W. of TRONES WOOD on N of MALTZ HORN VALLEY. 2nd i/c both Y3rd I.B. at BRIQUETERIE.	E.R.

WAR DIARY or INTELLIGENCE SUMMARY

Army Form C. 2118.

Place	Date	Hour	Summary of Events and Information	Remarks and references to Appendices
HAPPY VALLEY	18th	12.40 AM	Original disposition of guns as per attached. 18th I.B. OO. to say reed. altering Brigade attack to a two Battn. frontage & M.G. Reserve from four to six guns. Two guns attached to 9th R. Sussex Regt. detached from them & placed in Reserve at BRICQUETERIE.	
		5.30	Verbal message received from Sergt. Carter, that 2 LT ANDERSON's team had suffered severely & that the gun was out of action having been disabled by shell fire. Ordered Sergt Diarey to take forward one of his guns to replace damaged one, & for old team to report to Coy. Hd. Qrs.	
		6.30	Obtained leave from B.H.E. to replace Sergt Diarey's gun wi & his gun from Reserve, Cpl Evans & team sent forward. B.B. Action of guns now as attached.	
		8.0	ZERO time received, being 2.45 P.M.	
		8.55	Pte Swann i/c "B" gun team reported to C.H.Q. with gun & team having found himself in wrong assembly trenches & being unable to obtain	

WAR DIARY or INTELLIGENCE SUMMARY

Army Form C. 2118.

Place	Date	Hour	Summary of Events and Information	Remarks and references to Appendices
HAPPY VALLEY			13th Middx Regt. Any information from them to being ordered by them to report his Coy. Casualties up to this time. M.G.C. 2 Officers killed, shell fire. (2 Lt. F.L. BLECK & 2 Lt. G.R. ANDERSON) 2 O.R. killed, shell fire. 4 O.R. wounded, 2 O.R. missing. O.R. attached 4 wounded 2 missing.	
		2.45 PM	Attack started.	
		5.15	7th Batln (wounded) stated right Lewis gun held up with 13th Middlesex Regt. but going forward with Lewisters who were silencing them. Sergt. Cusly (wounded) stated the gun went forward & succeeded in establishing themselves 50 yds in front of line being consolidated by 7th Northampton shire Regt a about 100 yds to right of QUARRY	
		7.0 PM	Information recd through Maj Murphy (comp in command of 7th Northamptonshire) that his left flank was being covered by gun under Sergt. Disney who had succeeded in getting forward & establishing himself on his flank. TOTAL CASUALTIES for day: M.G.C. 2 Officers killed, 2 O.R. killed, 8 wounded, 2 missing. Attached O.R. 14 wounded, 4 missing.	

WAR DIARY or INTELLIGENCE SUMMARY

Army Form C. 2118.

Place	Date	Hour	Summary of Events and Information	Remarks and references to Appendices
HAPPY VALLEY	19"	1.25 AM	Received orders from Brig. Gen. to send one reserve gun to Quarry to report to Maj. Murphy. Sergt Simon + team set up but owing to lack of guides failed to get to position complete + returned to C/He Bn. 2nd R Lancs Regt. at gun under Sergt Huthard. relieved by Batn. of 72nd I.B.	
		10.0	Gun placed in reserve at BRIQUETERIE.	
		7.0 PM	Gun at Quarry relieved by 72nd M.G. Coy. no trace to be found of gun or team originally under Sergt Carter	
		10.0	2nd line guns under 2/Lts MAUNSELL & WOOD (Old 4) relieved by 4 guns of 105th Bde.	
		12.45	All guns relieved + moved to CARNOY CRATERS. under LT SPRINGFIELD. Casualties for day. 2/LT. DOVE WOUNDED gassed by gas-shell. Attached O.R's. Killed 1, Wounded 2, Sick to Hospital 1. Eight remaining guns in the line relieved by 72nd I.B. + brought to CARNOY CRATERS. under C.O. Coy.	R.T.R.
	20"	9 PM	Warning received from Bde that Coy. was in close reserve + must be ready to move at 15 minutes notice	

Army Form C. 2118.

WAR DIARY
or
INTELLIGENCE SUMMARY
(Erase heading not required.)

Instructions regarding War Diaries and Intelligence Summaries are contained in F. S. Regs., Part II. and the Staff Manual respectively. Title pages will be prepared in manuscript.

Place	Date	Hour	Summary of Events and Information	Remarks and references to Appendices
HAPPY VALLEY	21		Casualties for day. Attached O.R. wounded 1.	F.I
			1 O.R. attached from 13th Middlesex Regt. returned to his unit for dispatch being under age.	
			30 O.R. from Base Depot as reinforcements.	
			Received warning that Coy would be relieved by 60th M.G. Coy.	
	22.		Casualties M.G.C. O.R. wounded 2. Attached O.R. Sick to Hospital 3.	F.I
			1 O.R. discharged from Hospital.	
		11 AM	Relieved by 60th M.G. Coy. Coy moved to SAND PIT	
		5.30 PM	Warned to have 4 guns ready to go into the line again.	F.I
SAND PIT	23.		Line Relief by 105th M.G. Coy reconnoitred by LT. F.O. SPRINGFIELD	
		7.30 PM	No 3 Section under 2/LT TIBBITT took over from 106th M.G. Coy.	
			Relief greatly interfered with by heavy enemy shelling.	
			Casualties 1 O.R. wounded (shock, shell)	
	24.		Heavy shelling of front & support trenches by enemy.	F.I
			Casualties M.G.C. O.R. killed 2. wounded 1. Attached O.R. wounded 1.	
			Remainder of Coy. Reorganising & overhauling equipment.	

Army Form C. 2118.

WAR DIARY
or
INTELLIGENCE SUMMARY.
(Erase heading not required.)

Instructions regarding War Diaries and Intelligence Summaries are contained in F.S. Regs., Part II. and the Staff Manual respectively. Title pages will be prepared in manuscript.

Place	Date	Hour	Summary of Events and Information	Remarks and references to Appendices
SAND PIT	25		2 LT WOOD admitted to Hospital. accompanied by servant.	EDL
			18 I.B. moved to BUIRE.	
			Coy. received permission to move to HAPPY VALLEY to wait for relief. still in the line.	
		4.0 PM	Infantry Section in line informed by 106th Bde that they would be relieved that night.	
			C.O. 59th M.G. Coy reconnoitred line with a view to relieving all four guns	
		7.30	Relief started at 7.30 P.M. C.O. 59th M.G. Coy advised by his Brigade to only take over two guns as right Rand guns were in a line held by 35th Div.	
		8.0	Application made to 106th Bde to have two remaining guns relieved. Heavy shelling by enemy & counter attacks reported on right & left flanks.	
		10.0	106th M.G. Coy started to relieve two right Rand guns.	
			1 O.R. returned to duty from Hospital as officers servant.	
			Casualties 2 Lt. E. 1 O.R. wounded attached O.R. missing. 1 O.R. admitted Hospital.	

Army Form C. 2118.

WAR DIARY
or
INTELLIGENCE SUMMARY.
(Erase heading not required.)

Instructions regarding War Diaries and Intelligence Summaries are contained in F. S. Regs., Part II. and the Staff Manual respectively. Title pages will be prepared in manuscript.

Place	Date	Hour	Summary of Events and Information	Remarks and references to Appendices
HAPPY VALLEY			1. O.R. discharged Hospital.	
			6. O.R. transferred to K.G.C. from Bde Authy. Dw. g. e.R. No 18630/19/A.	EOL
	26.	3 am	dt-10/8/16. Relief completed in the line.	
		4.7pm	Coy marched with 2nd Leinster Regt to new Camp at BUIRE.	
			2. O.R. discharged Hospital.	ROL
BUIRÉ	27.	10.50	Address by Maj. Gen. Capper, Div Comdr, congratulating Bde on good work done in the line.	
			1. O.R. discharged Hospital.	
			LT G M SHANKS (5th Scottish Rifles) joined from Base Depot & taken on strength.	EOL
	28.		1. O.R. admitted Hospital	
			1. O.R. discharged Hospital.	
			39. O.R. Carries attached from Regt. returned to Units. Reorganising Coy, overhauling equipment. Preliminary notice that 13th I.B. would relieve a Bde of the 32nd Div.	

WAR DIARY
or
INTELLIGENCE SUMMARY.

(Erase heading not required.)

Army Form C. 2118.

Place	Date	Hour	Summary of Events and Information	Remarks and references to Appendices
BUIRE	29		in the line on night 31st August / 1st September.	EOS
			C.O. reconnoitred Line held by 98th M.G. Coy with a view to relieving them.	
			OO No 65 recd. ordering 93rd I.B. to relieve 98th I.B. in the line on night August 30/31st.	
			Disposition of guns to be. 8 in front line, 8 in close support, 6 in supports — 4 in reserve at Coy H.Q.	
			Coy H.Q. to be at POMMIERS REDOUBT.	
			I.O.R. reported from course colr. showing ABBEVILLE.	EOS
30.			93 M.G. Coy. O.O. No 6 issued (copy attached.)	
			Coy moved to POMMIERS REDOUBT afternoon + evening 930th.	
			Relief of 98 M.G. Coy delayed by weather conditions & heavy shelling.	
			6 guns in Savoy Trench under 2 LT F.A. PHILPOTT.	
			6 guns under 2 LT L. MAUNSELL + LT. G.M. SHANKS relived 6 forward guns of 98th as under, relief completed by 11 AM 31/8/16.	
			Front Line. No 1. About S.116.5.3. right of Middle line where PEACH TR.	

WAR DIARY
or
INTELLIGENCE SUMMARY

Army Form C. 2118.

Place	Date	Hour	Summary of Events and Information	Remarks and references to Appendices

RECORDED

Guns TEA TR.
No. 2. TEA TR. S11.b.05.
No. 3. S11.a.3.2. TEA.TR.
Support line
No. 4. Gun wrecked en route. Shovels &c. taken up position at
No. 5. Junction of ORCHARD TR. & WOOD LANE. about S11.a.10.8. ETT
S11.c.5.9.
Hd Qrs of 2/Lt MAUNSELL & LT SHANKS. near this gun.
No. 6. WOOD LANE approx. S11.a.3.0.
Four guns in Bde Reserve under 2Lt E. TIBBITT.
Enemy bombarded front system of trenches, till 3 PM & then attacked.
Events during bombardment preliminary to German attack
No. 1. All correct.
2. Gun, equipment & team blown up 2 men returned to Hd. Qrs.
3. All correct. Under orders from a MIDDX. battalion vacated
trench about 11 AM because shelling was so heavy, returned

WAR DIARY
or
INTELLIGENCE SUMMARY.

Army Form C. 2118.

Place	Date	Hour	Summary of Events and Information	Remarks and references to Appendices

BUZORDEL

to original position about 11-30 AM

No 4. non existent
5. all correct
6. all correct

Nos 7-12 correct in Sonny T.R.
Action during German attack.

No 1. Fired 1250 rounds at German Infantry coming up along Sea Sr. from the left. Rushed by bombers. Sergt 1/c destroyed gun with bomb. There were by that time no infantry left in trench. Sergt 1/c joined Sussex reinforcements & threw bombs. About 5 o'clock left Sussex & came back to Hd Qrs. Sergt 1/c reports his fire very effective but could not stop advance of bombers.

No. 2. non-existent

No. 3. Fired nearly a belt at German bombers coming down WOOD LANE. Shrapnel then put gun out of action.
While team then used rifles for about 20 minutes. Sergt 1/c asked to comment party of infantry during temporary absence of officer.

Army Form C. 2118.

WAR DIARY
or
INTELLIGENCE SUMMARY.
(Erase heading not required.)

Instructions regarding War Diaries and Intelligence Summaries are contained in F. S. Regs., Part II. and the Staff Manual respectively. Title pages will be prepared in manuscript.

Place	Date	Hour	Summary of Events and Information	Remarks and references to Appendices
BECORDEL			Sergt. & 2 men of team came back with damaged gun, tried to find support gun in ORCHARD TR with view to taking them up but failed, so came back to Coy	
			Hd Qrs. Damaged gun was repaired.	
			No 4. Non existent.	
			No 5. During German advance shell flew gun & all equipment completely away. Team under 2 Lt. MAUNSELL joined Middlesex & made a stand with rifles & bombs till reinforced by Leinsters. About 7.30 Sergt i/c collected N.C.C men & returned to Coy Hd Qrs.	
			No 6. About 2 o'clock Germans seen in TEA TR. NCO i/c expected frontal attack over open mounted gun accordingly. Germans came along WOOD LANE & appeared 30˟ away. Germans attempted to rush gun but its firing stopped first rush. Enemy reinforced by bombers, gun & equipment blown up. Team joined Middlesex & used rifles till reinforced by Leinsters. Team then returned to Hd Qrs.	
			C.O went forward at 4.30 PM to find out situation, moved two guns formed from Savoy Trench to the Pont Street to check any further advance	

T2134. Wt. W708—776. 500000. 4/15. Sir J. C. & S.

Army Form C. 2118.

WAR DIARY
or
INTELLIGENCE SUMMARY.
(Erase heading not required.)

Place	Date	Hour	Summary of Events and Information	Remarks and references to Appendices
BECORDEL			by enemy guns in Savoy Trench rearranged to meet altered situation. 1 gun in Savoy Trench put out of action by shrapnel & replaced by reserved gun. Firing done by guns in Savoy Trench. — A certain amount of night firing was done, traversing along SWITCH TR.	
	10		O.R. reinforcements from Base Depot. 29/8/16.	
	11		O.R. reinforcements " " 31/8/16.	
			1 O R discharged Hospital.	
			2 O R admitted Hospital.	
			Casualties. 2 LT. L.B. MAUNSELL Wounded (shell wound back)	
			☆ LT. G.M. SHANKS. do (shell wound right arm.)	
			O.R. killed 1, wounded 3.	
			Attached O.R. killed 1, wounded 1.	

Bich Col
Cmmny 3rd By

FIGHTING ORDER WILL BE AS FOLLOWS:-

Skeleton Order:-
  Full waterbottle.
  Haversack on back containing:-
    (a) Iron rations.
    (b) 1 pair of clean socks.

  4 sandbags slung through belt
  2 smoke helmets.
  2 bandoliers slung from shoulders.
  Steel helmet.
  2 bombs.(1 in each pocket)
  Nos. 1&2 will not carry rifles. They will as far
  as possible carry two short belts.

  Waterproof sheet.
  Canteen.
  Tomorrow's ration may be carried in one of the
  4 sandbags.

18/6/16.   (Signed) H.Gilbert,   Captain.

73 Company Machine Gun Corps.

ORDERS RE RELIEF. (17/8/16).

2nd Lieut Anderson responsible that his subsection joins Northamptons in left section trenches.(Route shown on most recent map). Guides for Northamptons will be at Briqetterie at 3 p.m. You will have a copy of map.

2nd Lieut Maunsell responsible that his forward subsection joins Sussex at Briqetterie about 4 p.m., and remain there with Sussex in dug-outs. This subsection to go up line with Sussex.

2nd Lieut Bleck's forward section is arranged for.

2nd Lieut Tibbitt with Pte Whitehall as guide to Briqetterie will leave camp about 3 p.m. and take up his positions, also point out Headquarter positions to C.S.M.

2nd Lieut Maunsell will leave camp about 3 p.m. and put in position second line subsections of No.2, No.4 and No.1 Sections as already pointed out.

2nd Lieut Anderson, Bleck, Sergt Searson, Disney, 2nd Lieut Maunsell, 2nd Lieut Wood will each have 2 orderlies from C.SM to go up with them. These orderlies will come back to report on relief to Lieut Springfield at La Briqatterie.

Sandbags containing each 10 rations can be had at Briqetterie. As many should be taken up as possible.

Second Line guns, Reserve Section and Headquarters may send back to Briqetterie for tools.

       (Signed)   H.Gilbert,   Captain,

Commanding 73 Company Machine Gun Corps.

73 Company, Machine Gun Corps.   16/8/16.

APPROXIMATE POSITIONS OF GUNS AND HEADQUARTERS.

No. 1 Section. "B" Gun advances.Right of Middlesex.R.2nd Lt Bleck.
"A" Gun   do   Left   do   do
"C" Gun S.30a.6.½.) 2nd Lieut Wood.
"D" Gun.S.30.c.6½.9½.) Indirect overhead fire S.E of GUILLEMONT.

No. 2 Section. "F" Gun advances Left of Northamptons.2/Lt Anderson.
"E" Gun   do   Right.   do.
"G" Gun.S.30.a.6.4½.) Direct overhead fire N.E of
"H" Gun.S.30.a.9.5½.) GUILLEMONT.

No. 4 Section. "O" Gun advances Left of R.Sussex R.
"P" Gun   do   Right.   do
"M" Gun.S.30.a.8½.3.) 2nd Lieut Maunsell.
"N" Gun.S.30.a.9.2½.) Direct overhead fire N.E. of GUILLEMONT.

No. 3 Section. Neighbourhood of S.29.d.10.2. 2 guns in each side of communication trench.Long range fire E. of GUILLEMONT. Mobile reserve.

Company Headquarters. Neighbourhood of S.29.d.5.0.

Brigade Battle Headquarters. Briqetterie.A.4.b.7.2.

                    (Signed) H.Gilbert, Captain.

Position of guns at 8AM 18/8/16

No 1 Section	Front guns	Normal
	2nd line	Normal
2 "	Front guns	1 in position
		1 out of action but replaced by 2nd line gun.
	2nd line	1 in position.
		1 sent forward to front line. but replaced by gun of No 4 Sect.
3 "	Complete Sect.	Normal.
4 "	2nd line	Normal
	Reserve	1 normal
		1 sent forward to replace No 2 Sect. gun in 2nd line

R Spry

SECRET.   73 Coy, M.Gun Corps. O.O.No. 6 30/8/16.

1. 73 M.Gun Coy will relieve 98 M.Gun Coy in afternoon of 30th and night 30th-31st Aug. Maps showing Brigade area have already been distributed. Move as per attached table.
2. Route for all parties will be as follows:-
    QUARRY(E.14.c)-DERNANCOURT-MEAULTE-CARCAILLOT FARM- level crossing F.9.a.6.8½-MAMETZ-POMMIERS REDOUBT.
    If dry weather tracks are passable they will be used as much as possible.
3. The march will take about 3 hours. An additional 1½ hours has been allowed in the table to allow for 1st party to halt for dinners and other parties for teas. Halts for this purpose must be well off the roads, limbers included
4. No.3 Section will detail 1 junior N.C.O and one man to take over the company water and ration dump at GREEN DUMP.
5. Company Headquarters will be at POMMIERS REDOUBT.
6. 2nd Lieut Tibbitt will comply with orders re packs as in "ADMINISTRATIVE ARRANGEMENTS".
7. On completion of reliefs transport will return to present lines.
8. Lieut Springfield will remain at present camp until all details have removed to new area.
9. Guides for SAVOY TRENCH party will be at POMMIERS REDOUBT. Guides for the 6 forward guns will be arranged later. They will probably be in SAVOY TRENCH.
10. As per instructions already issued 2 men per gun return to report on relief.
11. All other details will be communicated direct.

Date.	Party	Starting Point.	Time.	To be at POMMIERS REDOUBT at	Guns to be relieved.	Remarks.
30th	Subsections of:- No 4(Sgt Searson) No.2 " Disney No 1 " Hubbard. With 3 Fighting Limbers.	Present Camp.	10 a.m.	2-30 p.m	6 guns in SAVOY TRENCH Relief by day to be over as soon as possible.	Minimum teams only. Remainder of these subsections to be attached to No. 3 Section.
30th	ditto. (Remaining subsections. 3 Fighting Limbers.	Ditto.	2 p.m	6-30 p.m	3 Guns in front line 3 guns in support line. as per attached map.	Minimum teams only. Remainder of these subsections to be attached to No 3 Section.
30th	No 3 Sect. & attached with 2 fighting limbers.	Ditto.	4 p.m.	Destination and time to be noified later.	To be in reserve.	

73rd Brigade.
24th Division.

73rd MACHINE GUN COMPANY

SEPTEMBER 1916

Herewith please find War Diary
complete for the month of September
from 93 Coy Machine Gun Corps.
Delay regretted.

K. Gillart.
Major
~~Captain~~
COMMANDING No.   M.G. COY.,
MACHINE GUN CORPS.

73 M.G. Coy 2-4 Army Form C. 2118.

VOL 6

WAR DIARY
INTELLIGENCE SUMMARY.
(Erase heading not required.)

Place	Date	Hour	Summary of Events and Information	Remarks and references to Appendices
BECORDEL	Sept. 1.		Bombing attack against enemy holding PLUM ALLEY. Guns could not co-operate.	
		2 P.M	Gun moved from PONT STREET to support right flank of Lewis's Regt. in WORCESTER TRENCH.	
			4 guns of 19th M.G Coy came into the line, two in ORCHARD TRENCH and two in SAVOY TRENCH.	
			Casualties:- O.R. Killed 1. Wounded 5. Missing 6.	
			Attached O.R. Killed 1. 2 O.R admitted Hospital.	
	2.		Orders received from B.G.C. to send a gun forward to protect left flank of Sussex Regt. The gun took up a position in PEACH TRENCH about 20 ft behind.	E/.
			During the 1st & 2nd guns in SAVOY TRENCH fired on small parties of the enemy in the vicinity of the IRON GATE.	

WAR DIARY
or
INTELLIGENCE SUMMARY

Army Form C. 2118.

Place	Date	Hour	Summary of Events and Information	Remarks and references to Appendices
BECORDEL			Received orders that for B.G.C. that Coy would be relieved by 14 Coy & G.C.	
			Relief commenced at 5:30 PM & completed at 2 AM 2/9/16.	
			Position of guns when relieved by 14th Coy.	
			1 gun PEACH TRENCH	
			1 " PONT STREET	
			1 " WORCESTER TRENCH.	ED
			~~ORCHARD TRENCH~~	
			3 " SAVOY TRENCH.	
			4 " QUARRY S22.C.0.5.	
			2 O.R. admitted Hospital	
			1 O.R. returned from course of instruction at M.G. School CAMIERS	
			2LT A.J.K. DAVIS & 2LT W.M. WHITWORTH joined Coy from Base Depot & taken on strength.	ED
	2.		Coy warned by Brigade that they must be ready to move at 30 mins notice. Coy reorganized & teams formed for all available guns.	ED

Army Form C. 2118.

WAR DIARY
or
INTELLIGENCE SUMMARY
(Erase heading not required.)

Instructions regarding War Diaries and Intelligence Summaries are contained in F.S. Regs., Part II. and the Staff Manual respectively. Title pages will be prepared in manuscript.

Place	Date	Hour	Summary of Events and Information	Remarks and references to Appendices
BELLORDEL	4.		24 Division wired warning Coy that it might be required to assist the 14th Bde in holding the line	
			2 LT. C.T.A SANDERSON joined Coy from Base Depot & taken on strength.	
			1 O.R. joined Coy from Base Depot & taken on strength	
			2 LT. E.M. TIBBITT & 3 O.R. to CAMIERS for course of instruction at M.G. School.	
			Preliminary move order rec'd. from Bde. & that the Coy would move to billets	
			in DERNANCOURT on following day.	
			25 O.R. 9th reinforcements from Base Depot.	
			1 O.R. admitted Hospital	
		12.30 PM	Order Rec'd from Bde to send 1 N.C.O. & 3 O.R. to Y2 I.B. at once"	
		1 PM	Cpl. Goodfellow & 3 O.R. sent to Y2 I.B.	
			2 O.R. reported missing 15/7/16 now reported wounded.	
	5.		Coy marched to billets in DERNANCOURT. G.S. waggon did not accompany it.	E.D.
			Men carried full marching order.	
			Rec'd orders from Bde that Coy would entrain at EDGE HILL at 8 AM	
ERNANCOURT			destination LONGPRÉ	

T2134. Wt. W708-776. 500000. 4/15. Sir J.C. & S.

WAR DIARY
INTELLIGENCE SUMMARY

Army Form C. 2118.

Place	Date	Hour	Summary of Events and Information	Remarks and references to Appendices
DERNANCOURT	6.		Transport Brigaded under CAPT. FOWLER. BT.O. to march by road. Coy drew two days rations which were issued to men. Entrained at EDGE HILL at 9AM. Detrained at LONGPRÉ. Marched to BOUCHONS & billetted there.	EDL
BOUCHONS	7.		1 O.R. discharged Hospital. Coy Kit inspection.	EDL
	8.	8PM	Transport arrived under 2LT T.H. BELL. LT E.B. MILLER & 2LT P.M. ANDREWS joined as reinforcements from BaseDepot & taken on strength	EDL
	9.		Overhauling equipment, gun material & limbers. Reorganising Coy into teams & allotting new guns. Packing of limbers.	EDL
	10.		Examination of all recent reinforcements. 1 O.R. admitted Hospital 9/9/16. 1 O.R. do do 10/9/16 6 hours Infantry training & M.G. Drill.	EDL

Army Form C. 2118.

WAR DIARY
or
INTELLIGENCE SUMMARY.
(Erase heading not required.)

Instructions regarding War Diaries and Intelligence Summaries are contained in F.S. Regs., Part II. and the Staff Manual respectively. Title pages will be prepared in manuscript.

Place	Date	Hour	Summary of Events and Information	Remarks and references to Appendices
BOUCHON.	11.		1 O.R. discharged Hospital. 6 hours infantry training, M.G. Drill & Commencing M.G. Range NW of village.	KD
	12		4 hours work on Range which was completed. 2 hours work Advanced Drill.	KD
	13.		6 O.R. admitted Hospital. 4 following	KD
			10 O.R. transferred to 92 M.C. Coy. authy. 94th Div. NoA/2130/31 dated 11/9/16. 10 O.R. " " 19 M.G. Coy } (43 I.B. SCA 19 a/- 11/9/16). No 1 Section testing new reinforcements in stoppages on Range. Remaining section 6 hours training	
	14		No 2 Section testing new reinforcements in stoppages on Range Remaining Coy Route march under 2LT SPRINGFIELD.	KD
	15		hrs 3 & 4 Sections work as above on Range hrs 1 & 2 Advanced drill 2LT DAVIS & 2LT PHILPOTT 48 hours leave to PARIS.	KD

T2134. Wt. W708—776. 500000. 4/16. Sir J.C. & S.

Army Form C. 2118.

WAR DIARY
or
INTELLIGENCE SUMMARY.
(Erase heading not required.)

Instructions regarding War Diaries and Intelligence Summaries are contained in F. S. Regs., Part II. and the Staff Manual respectively. Title pages will be prepared in manuscript.

Place	Date	Hour	Summary of Events and Information	Remarks and references to Appendices
BOUCHON	16.		Lieut E.O Springfield Leave to U.K. 20.R Discharged Hospital	
	17		6608 C.Q.M.S. Shivas C. and 6616 Sergt Mulland Leave to U.K.	
	18.		2nd Lt Davis and 2nd Lt Philpot reported on expiration of Leave to France.	
	18		Company had orders to move the following day. 1.Q.R admitted Hospital	
	19.		Company left in two parties. 1st party, Transport and all Old Company men moved off at 7.20 A.M. 2nd party moved off at 9-15 A.M. Both parties marched to Longpré and entrained at 10 A.M Train left Longpré at 12.45 p.m. Company detrained at FOUQUEREIL at 7.15 p.m. Company left Fouquereil station at 8 p.m and marched to MARLES EZ MINES arriving there 10-30 p.m.	
	19.		6642 Sergt. H. Disney Leave to U.K.	
Marles Ez Mines	20		Resting and overhauling equipment	
Marles Ez Mines	21.		Company received orders from Brigade to proceed to HOUDAIN opposite branch company left MARLES EZ MINES at 10.10 A.M arriving HOUDAIN 12.30 p.m.	

Army Form C. 2118.

WAR DIARY
or
INTELLIGENCE SUMMARY.
(Erase heading not required.)

Instructions regarding War Diaries and Intelligence Summaries are contained in F. S. Regs., Part II. and the Staff Manual respectively. Title pages will be prepared in manuscript.

Place	Date	Hour	Summary of Events and Information	Remarks and references to Appendices
MARLES LES MINES	21		"C" Company with 2nd Lt Whitworth and Andrew recognitred line to be taken over from 26th Machine gun company.	MBM.
HOUDAIN	22		Company received orders from Brigade to proceed to CAMBLAIN L'ABBE by route march. Company left HOUDAIN 7-30 AM arrived at CAMBLAIN L'ABBE 11-30 AM and relieved 26 Machine gun company in billets.	MBM.
	22		Lt Miller & 2 nos Philpott and Davis recognitred the line to be taken over from the 28th Machine Gun Company.	MBM.
	22		2nd Lt Whitworth with No 3 Section relieved 4 guns of 26th Machine Gun Company in BAJOLLE SWITCH relief completed 9pm. 1 Gun of No 4 Section and 1 gun No 2 Section relieved 2 guns of the 26. Machine gun Company relief completed 10pm. Seven guns dump under guard at CABARET ROUGE DUMP at 9pm.	MBM.
	22		1 O.R. Proceeded on leave to U.K.	MBM.
	22		1 O.R. previously reported missing 31/5/16 now reported killed in action	MBM.

T2134. Wt. W708—776. 500000. 4/15. Sir J. C. & S.

WAR DIARY
or
INTELLIGENCE SUMMARY.
(Erase heading not required.)

Army Form C. 2118.

Place	Date	Hour	Summary of Events and Information	Remarks and references to Appendices
AMBLAIN L'ABBE	23		Two teams No 4 Section and 4 teams No 1 Sections and 3 teams No 2 Section pushed 2.15 am to relieve remaining guns of No 26 Machine Gun Company. Relief started 9 AM completed 11 AM.	
	23		No 3 Section in BAIELLE SWITCH relieved by + guns of No 72nd Machine Gun Company and returned to Company HQ	
	23		1 OR proceeded on leave to U.K. 2/Lt E.M. TIBBITT	
	23		1 OR and 3 ORs rejoined Company from Machine Gun School at CAMIERS. Company received orders to move by Brigade to proceed to GOUY-SERVINS and hand over our billets at CAMBLAIN L'ABBE to 17th Machine Gun Company	
"	24		Company marched to GOUY-SERVINS and reached there at 4 pm	
	25		2 ORs admitted to hospital	
	"		1 OR proceeded to Machine Gun School CAMIERS	
	"		1 OR leave to proceed to U.K.	
GOUY-SERVINS	26		Company received orders to move Company HQ to VILLERS-AU-BOIS. Transport to move to PT SERVINS. Company moved VILLERS-AU-BOIS at 4 pm	

Army Form C. 2118.

WAR DIARY
or
INTELLIGENCE SUMMARY.
(Erase heading not required.)

Instructions regarding War Diaries and Intelligence Summaries are contained in F. S. Regs., Part II. and the Staff Manual respectively. Title pages will be prepared in manuscript.

Place	Date	Hour	Summary of Events and Information	Remarks and references to Appendices
VILLERS-AUBEIS	27.		N°6615 Sergt Carter awarded Distinguished Conduct Medal for distinguished conduct in the field on 17th August 1916.	9thMr
	27		Temporary Captain H Gilbert appointed Temporary Superintendent commanding Company dated 14th July 1916.	9thMr
			1 O.R. admitted to Hospital	9thMr
			1 Officer proceeded on leave to U.K. 1 Gun Reg Section sent to the line	9thMr
	28.		1 Gun Team took over new position on the line. 1 Gun Team	9thMr
	29		returned to Company H.Q. of N°2 Section	9thMr
			1 O.R. proceeded on leave to U.K.	9thMr
	29		1 O.R. proceeded on leave to U.K.	9thMr
	30		1 O.R. discharged from Hospital	9thMr
			1 Gun team N°3 Section into trenches to take over new gun position in front line instead of 2nd Divn.	9thMr

Robert Nyn
Comndg 73 M.G.Coy.

73rd Brigade.
24th Division.

73rd MACHINE GUN COMPANY

OCTOBER 1 9 1 6.

M/3 L.B

Herewith War Diary (original)
for my Coy for the month of October
1916.

E.W.Cooper 2/Lt for Major
O.C. 73 Coy M.G. Corps

Vol 7

Army Form C. 2118.

WAR DIARY or INTELLIGENCE SUMMARY

1/3rd M.G. Coy   October 1916

(Erase heading not required.)

Instructions regarding War Diaries and Intelligence Summaries are contained in F.S. Regs., Part II. and the Staff Manual respectively. Title pages will be prepared in manuscript.

Place	Date	Hour	Summary of Events and Information	Remarks and references to Appendices
VILLERS-AU-BOIS	Oct 1.		1 O.R. leave to U.K.	ETD
	2.		2 O.R. admitted Hospital.	
			In conjunction with 68th M.G. Coy all enemy track areas kept under fire during night rounds fired 22,000.	
			Enemy front line & wiring parties fired upon by movable gun in front line rounds fired 2,000.	ETD
	3.		2 O.R. discharged Hospital.	
			Minenwerfer firing from edge of BOIS DE GIVENCHY fired on by gun from Quarry. rounds fired 1,000.	
			Wiring party fired on by front line gun. probable casualties two men & two stretcher bearers.	
			By request of O. 9th R. Sussex Regt. fired upon enemy post on edge of crater, in morning structure observed to be damaged & trip alarm away.	RTD
			1 O.R. proceeded to join M.G. Base Depot ETAPLES on instructions received from D.A.G. Base. Being surplus to establishment.	
	4		During night M/5th all roads, tracks & tramways kept under organised	

Army Form C. 2118.

WAR DIARY
or
INTELLIGENCE SUMMARY.
(Erase heading not required.)

Instructions regarding War Diaries and Intelligence Summaries are contained in F. S. Regs., Part II. and the Staff Manual respectively. Title pages will be prepared in manuscript.

Place	Date	Hour	Summary of Events and Information	Remarks and references to Appendices
VILLERS AU BOIS	5.		fire from sio guns rounds fired 26,950. 1 O.R. admitted Hospital.	RTD
	6.		1 O.R. leave to UK 6/15th	RTD
	7.		Raid carried out by 2nd Rennets Regt. supported by 2 Vickers guns under 2/Lt A.J.K.DAVIS. Simultaneously, between 30-40 Germans seen advancing towards our line. Both Vickers opened on them & a large number seen to fall. Lt Regt up intermittently by these two guns for about 30 mins. Early morning of 8th trench sentries reported noises as if enemy were carrying away dead & wounded. At daylight 8 dead Germans were seen in the wire. These guns fired 1650 rounds.	RTD
	8.		Military cross awarded to 2/Lt L.B. MAUNSELL 8th S. Staffords Regt. att 153rd M.G. Coy. (DRO 1596. 8/10/16.) 1 O.R. wounded, slightly at duty. (admitted to Hospital 10F)	RTD
	9.		1 O.R. leave to U.K. 9/18th. Enemy raid expected & fresh Lewis gun trench by two extra Vickers guns. Raid by 4th Northampton Regt. covered by two guns of the Coy.	RTD

WAR DIARY
INTELLIGENCE SUMMARY

Army Form C. 2118.

Place	Date	Hour	Summary of Events and Information	Remarks and references to Appendices
VILLERS-AU-BOIS	10		1 O.R. discharged Hospital.	
	11.		Relieved in the line by 17th Inf. Coy. OC. Hoy attacked.	
			Coy. moved to rest billets in CAMBLAIN L'ABBÉ on completion of relief	
	12.		1 O.R. admitted to Hospital.	
			1 O.R. discharged. Hospital.	
	13.		Major H. GILBERT leave to U.K. 13/9/27. Two officers sent to reconnoitre new line.	
	14.		1 O.R. returned to duty from R.G. Petrol Carriers. 1 O.R. admitted Hospital.	
	15.		Two officers sent to reconnoitre new line.	
	16.		Two R.E. reconnoitred O.C. & 1 officer. Church Parade. Constructing service range & putting all Nos. 1 & 2 through Revolver Practice.	
	17.		One having bombing tench. putting all Nos. 3 & 4 through 7 days bombing course. Section Officers & Sergts. reconnoitred line to be taken over by their respective sections.	

WAR DIARY
or
INTELLIGENCE SUMMARY.
(Erase heading not required.)

Army Form C. 2118.

Place	Date	Hour	Summary of Events and Information	Remarks and references to Appendices
CAMBLAIN L'ABBÉ	19.		14 Guns & equipment sent forward to CENTRAL DUMP by train from BRAY WOOD under Lieut Ruttley as per O.O. No 3.	XII
	19		"A" Coy relieved the 1/2nd H.L. Coy in the BERTHONVAL SECTOR as per Operation Order No 8 attached. Relief Completed by 12 M.N.	XII
	20.		Positions of two guns altered so as to completely cnr ZOUAVES VALLEY. Indirect night fire brought to bear upon DUMP located by R.F.C. on previous day.	XII
	21.		2.LT C.W. SCOTT 13th R WAR.R. joined from Base.	XII
	22.		Large working party caught by gun under 2.LT A.J.K. DAVIS & dispersed. Sniping very active guns in front had fired at flashes & obtained hits on armour plates 6,750 rds fired.	XII
	23.		1 O.R. died at 23 C.C.S. 2. O.R. leave to U.K.	XII

Army Form C. 2118.

WAR DIARY
or
INTELLIGENCE SUMMARY.
(Erase heading not required.)

Instructions regarding War Diaries and Intelligence Summaries are contained in F.S. Regs., Part II. and the Staff Manual respectively. Title pages will be prepared in manuscript.

Place	Date	Hour	Summary of Events and Information	Remarks and references to Appendices
CAMBLAIN L'ABBE	25		Lt. E.O. SPRINGFIELD proceeded to M.G.T.C. Catterick AG/A 6664 7/10/16) 2nd Lt. C.E.R. CROAKER joined from 63rd M.G.Coy (Authy A.G. AM/767) 18/10/16 and appointed second-in-command. Two officers sent to reconnoitre new line.	C&RG
"	26		3rd Canadian M.G.Coy arrive to take over billets. Relieved in line by 3rd Canadian M.G.Coy.	C&RG
"	27		Operation Order attached (No. 9). Relief completed by 12 noon. O.C. + 1 officer reconnoitre new line. 26 men transferred from units in the Brigade to the 93rd M.G.Coy (authy. 1st Army 341 (G)	C&RG
"	28		Notification of new establishment. (Extra 32 men, 1 G.S. Wagon, 1 Driver, 2 Heavy slings) authy. 1st Army No. 341 (G) Company move to MAZINGARBE	C&RG
MAZINGARBE	28		Coy relieved 119th M.G.Coy in the LOOS SECTION. (Operation Order No.9 attached) 70 men + 14 guns sent into the line	C&RG

T2134. Wt. W708—776. 500000. 4/15. Sir J.C.&S.

Army Form C. 2118.

WAR DIARY
or
INTELLIGENCE SUMMARY.
(Erase heading not required.)

Instructions regarding War Diaries and Intelligence Summaries are contained in F. S. Regs., Part II. and the Staff Manual respectively. Title pages will be prepared in manuscript.

Place	Date	Hour	Summary of Events and Information	Remarks and references to Appendices
MAZINGARBE	29		Relief completed by 11.45 P.M. Coy. H.Q. in MAZINGARBE.	C&L.g
LES BREBIS	31		Coy. H.Q. moved into billets at LES BREBIS arriving 10.0 AM. One gun fired 500 rounds from open emplacement into german front line during night. Received new Pattern Box Respirators (small) from H.4. M.G.S.	C&L.g

H. Nixent. Major.
O.C. No 73 Coy M Gun Corps.

T2134. Wt. W708—776. 500000. 4/15. Sir J. C. & S.

SECRET.   COPY NO 2

73rd Company, Machine Gun Corps.

OPERATION ORDER No. 7.

Coy. H. Q. October 10th 1916.

On the day of the 11th and night 11th/12th the 73rd Machine Gun Company will be relieved in the trenches of the CARENCY SECTION by the 17th Machine Gun Company.

1. Nos. 1, 9, 7 & 12 guns will ne withdrawn and Nos. 2, 3, 5 & 8, BAJOLLE left, BAJOLLE right, and No. 11 will be relieved on the morning of the 11th. All guns and gun equipment will be dumped at WILKES WALK and relieve teams will be marched to Coy. H. Q.

Nos. 2, 3, 5, 8 & 11 BAJOLLE LEFT f BAJOLLE RIGHT will each leave 12 belt boxes in their emplacements, if these are not already there they must be withdrawn from the store at WILKES WALK. All ammunition belonging to guns No. 1, 9, 7, & 12 will be dumped at WILKES WALK.

2. GUIDES

Guides for BAJOLLE LEFT and BAJOLLE RIGHT will report to Officers Mess at 8-45 a.m.

The guide to WILKES WALK will report to Officers Mess at 9-15 a.m.

The guides for 6 & 10 will report to Officers Mess at 4-45 p.m.

All the above to be detailed by the C.SM.

Guides from Nos. 2, 3, 5, 8 & 11 to be at WILKES WALK at 10 a.m. and wait there for incoming teams.

3. HANDING OVER

N.C.O's i/c teams must make very effort to hans over as completely as possible, important points are; Ration arrangements and position of team dump, Position of water supply, Trench map, which must be handed over, standing orders and information about Infantry dispositions. Every dugout and emplacement must be left scrupulously clean.

4. OFFICERS RESPONSIBILITIES.

Officers will supervise withdrawal or relief of teams as follows:-

2nd/Lt. Philpott relief of No. 8 & withdrawal of Nos 9 & 7 (commencing 9 a.m.)

Lt. Miller relief of 2, 3, 5 & 11 and withdrawal of No 12 (commencing at 9 a.m.)

2nd/Lt Sanderson relief of Nos 6 & 10 on night of 11th/12th BAJOLLE LEFT and BAJOLLE RIGHT and WILKES WALK.

5. TIMES OF RELIEVING TEAMS ARRIVAL.

The relieving teams will arrive at guns positions at approximately the following times :-

BAJOLLE LEFT & RIGHT   10-30 a.m.
No. 8 & 11.   12 noon.
Nos. 2, 3 & 5.   11 a.m.
No 6 & 10.   6-30 p.m.

6. AMMUNITION.

No belt boxes will be brought out of the line, all surplus to 12 per relieved gun will dumped at WILKES WALK. Private Clay & team will remain at WILKES WALK until all guns and equipment are loaded on to limbers. Officers & N.C.O's must be careful to see that company equipment in the way of saw etc are not left behind as trench stores

(Continued)

8. TRANSPORT REQUIREMENTS.
   2 mules for 1 gun limber at 8-30 a.m.
   2 : : : : :   : 4-30 p.m.
   2 : : : : :   : 5-0 p.m.
   8 : for 2 Ammunition limbers at 5-0 p.m.

Issued at 5 p.m.

              E O Springfield
               for Major,
Commanding 73rd Company, Machine Gun Corps.

  Copy No. 1. File.
       2. War Diary.
       3. C.O.
       4.&5 17th Machine Gun Company.
       6&7 Transport Officer.
       8. 2/Lt. Tibbitt.
       9. 2/Lt. Philpott.
      10. Lt. Miller.
      11. 2/Lt. Sanderson.
      12. No. 6 gun.
      13. No. 10 gun.
      14. C.S.M.
      15. C.Q.M.S.

SECRET
Ref. Maps.
36.B.S.E.
1/20,000
& Trench
Maps.

73rd Machine Gun Company.

Copy No. 2

OPERATION ORDER No. 8.

October 18th 1916.

1. The 73rd M.G.Company will relieve the 72nd M.G.Coy. in the BERTHONVAL SECTION on October 19th as per attached table. Team commanders are responsible that all precautions are taken to conceal movement during the relief.

2. BOYAU 123 and WORTLEY AVENUE will be used as UP communication trenches.

3. All teams will send up their guns and equipment by limber leaving CAMBLAIN at 2 p.m. for BRAY WOOD and thence by train to CENTRAL DUMP.

4. Teams will march to CENTRAL DUMP as per attached table.

5. Packs will be packed on G.S.Wagon by 7 a.m. 19th inst and carried thus as far as CARENCY.

6. Nos. 2 & 3 sections will pack their remaining guns on a gun limber which will leave CAMBLAIN for POINT "G" at 5 p.m. 19th inst. Sgt. Raithby and CPL. Mahon will arrange to have this limber met and get their guns etc.

7. **RATIONS.**

    Rations will come by train nightly to the following dumps

Ration Men.	Dump.	Time.	Teams rationed.
Cpl. Batchelor.	CENTRAL.	6-30 p.m.	All teams except Nos. 6 & 7.
	GRANBY.	8-45. p.m.	6 & 7.
Pte. Buss.	CABARET ROUGE.	8-0. p.m.	T.H.Q. & Coy. Reserve.

Water is drawn from supplies at ZOUAVE VALLEY and CABARET ROUGE. ~~Teams must take care~~
Teams must make sure that the outgoing teams leave petrol cans.

8. **REPORTS.**
    Reports and letters from positions Nos. 1 to 8 will be at Officers dugout CENTRAL DUMP by 9 a.m. daily thence by runner to T.H.Q.
    Those from Nos. 9 to 14 positions & Coy. Reserve will go direct to T.H.Q. and be thereby 10 a.m.
    Runner leaves T.H.Q. at 10-30 a.m. daily for POINT "G".
    A mounted orderly will be at POINT "G" at 11 a.m. daily to take reports to C.H.Q.
    Mounted orderly will leave C.H.Q. 7 a.m. daily for POINT "G" and be met by runner from T.H.Q.

9. Officers i/c sections will report relief complete to T.H.Q. Every effort will be made to complete relief by 12 noon 19th inst.

10. Coy. H.Q. will be at CAMBLAIN l'ABBE.
    Trench Head Quarters will be at CABARET ROUGE.

11. Lists of trench stores etc taken over will be sent to T.H.Q. by 10 a.m. the 20th inst.

Issued at 2 p.m.

E.O.Springs___ for Major.
Commanding 73rd Company, Machine Gun Corps.

TIME TABLE ISSUED WITH 73rd MACHINE GUN COMPANY OPERATION ORDER No. 8.

Unit.	Time of Departure.	In relief of.	To.
No. 1. Section.	7-30 a.m.	Guns. No. 1,2,8 & 9.	CENTRAL DUMP.
No. 2. :	-:do:-	: No. 3,4,5.	-:do:-
No. 3. :	-:do:-	: No. 10,11,12.	-:do:-
No. 4. :	-:do:-	: No. 6,7,13,14.	-:do:-
T.H.Q.	8 a.m.	72nd. T. H. Q.	CABARET ROUGE.
Coy. Reserve under 2/Lt. Philpott.	9 a.m.	------	BAJOLLE LINE.

```
Copy No. 1.     File.
        2 & 3.  War Diary.
        4 & 5.  72nd Machine Gun Company.
        6 & 7.  Transport Officer.
        8.      Lt. Springfield.
        9.      Lt. Miller.
        10.     2/Lt. Philpott.
        11.       ;    Sanderson.
        12.       :    Tibbitt.
        13.       :    Andrews.
        14.     Sgt. Searson.
        15.       :    Raithby.
        16.     C.Q.M.S.
```

73rd Machine Gun Company   Copy No......

OPERATION ORDER No 9.

1. The 73rd Machine Gun Company will be relieved by the 3rd Canadian Machine Gun Company on the morning of the 26th inst. Their guns, equipment etc, will come up with tonights ration train and will be dumped at CENTRAL DUMP and a guard placed over them.

2. **GUIDES**

Guides for each gun team will be at CENTRAL DUMP at 10 a.m.
One guide to be at HOSPITAL CORNER at 9 a.m. to lead all the incoming teams up to CENTRAL DUMP. (Sgt. Raithby to detail a reliable man for this job).
One guide to be at CABARET ROUGE, T.H.Q. at 9-30 a.m. to guide the reserve men of the incoming company to our company reserve dugout in COLISEUM. Sgt. Searson to detail a man from T.H.Q. for this job.

3. **GUNS ETC.**

All guns and gun equipment will be dumped by each team as they are relieved at CENTRAL DUMP and Sgt. Raithby and six men will act as guard on the dump until the evening. When they will load the guns etc on to trucks in the ration train and come back with it. They will be met by our limbers at BRAY WOOD JUNCTION.

4. **AMMUNITION.**

10 belt boxes full will be left in each emplacement and all S.A.A. in bulk. The remainder of the belt boxes will be brought out and dumped with the guns etc.

5. **TRENCH STORES.**

Section Officers will hand over all Trench Stores which they took over from the 72nd M.G.Coy. and will bring back a list signed by the officer to whom they have handed over.

6. **DUGOUTS.**

All dugouts and emplacements will be left clean.

7. **AFTER RELIEF.**

After being relieved the sections having dumped their guns etc will be marched back independently to CAMBLAIN l'ABBE by section sergeants. Officers in charge of sections will report relief of their sections at T.H.Q. CABARET ROUGE.

8. **HORSES.**

Officers horses will be at HOSPITAL CORNER at 11 a.m. and will wait there till the officers come for them.

Issued at 10-30 a.m.   Lt. for Major,

                      Commanding 73rd Company, Machine Gun Corps.

Copy No.		
1.		File.
2 & 3.		War Diary.
4.		3rd Canadian M.G.Company.
5.& 6.		Transport Officer.
7.		Major Gilbert.
8.		Lt. Miller.
9.		2/Lt. Tibbitt.
10.	:	Sanderson.
11.	:	Andrews.
12.	:	Davis.
13.	Sgt.	Searson.
14.	:	Raithby.
15.		C.Q.M.S.

O.O. No 10

RELIEF ORDERS for NIGHT of October 28/29/16.

1. The 73rd M.G.Coy. will relieve the 119th M.G.Coy in the LOOS SECTOR.

2. The 119th M.G.Coy. will provide guides as follows :-
(a) From gun teams in the line.
R.30. R31. R.32. R.33. (1 per gun) will be at HATCHETTS at 7 p.m.
R.23. R.25. S.11. S.12. S.13. (1 per gun) will be at R.23. at 6-45 p.m.
S.14. S.15. R.27. R.28. R.29. will be at the ruined house near junction of LENS and MAROC road where the sentry stands at 6-30 p.m.

(b) From Corps in billets.
Guides will be at 73rd M.G.Coy. H.Qrs. MAZINGARBE at 5 p.m.
They will guide the transport and gun teams of the 73rd M.G.Coy. up the LENS road to the unloading place, and hand over the teams to the guides mentioned in para 2 (a) except that the transport, and teams for R.23 will proceed via LES BREBIS and MAROC.

73rd Brigade.
24th Division.

73rd MACHINE GUN COMPANY.

NOVEMBER 1916.

73rd Brigade.
24th Division.

73rd MACHINE GUN COMPANY.

NOVEMBER 1916.

Army Form C. 2118.

WAR DIARY
or
INTELLIGENCE SUMMARY.
(Erase heading not required.)

Instructions regarding War Diaries and Intelligence Summaries are contained in F. S. Regs., Part II. and the Staff Manual respectively. Title pages will be prepared in manuscript.

Place	Date	Hour	Summary of Events and Information	Remarks and references to Appendices

Vol 8

4th Warwickshire Gun Company

War Diary for month of November 1916

WAR DIARY
or
INTELLIGENCE SUMMARY.
(Erase heading not required.)

Army Form C. 2118.

Place	Date	Hour	Summary of Events and Information	Remarks and references to Appendices
LES BREBIS	1/11/16		Received new Box Respirators (Small)	C&CC
"	2.		1 ordinary Rank discharged from Hospital	
			Fired 1000 into Enemy's support trench from 10.0 pm to 4.0 AM, also	
"	3.		2750 rounds into fros hers B from 6.0 pm to 3.30 AM	
			Fired 1500 rounds at Enemy's Ration dumps, also 2000 rds short	
			feet hair road.	C&CC
"	4.		2 ordinary Ranks returned from Brigadier gun School St Omin	C&CC
"	5.		2 men sent to Base school (over establishment) Authy. A.G. N° C.R. N° 146/2/67	
			C date 27/10/16	
			Section	
"	6.		Inter Coy relief on the line, as per operation order N° 11 attached	C&CC
			1 on discharged from Hospital	
			1 new men transferred to the Company from the Infantry Regs of the	
			Brigade.	
			1 Officer 1 ordinary rank proceeded to the Brigade gun School Camin	
			1 O.R. admitted to Hospital	C&CC
"	7		50 OR fitted and tested with new Box Respirator	
"	9		60 OR " " " " " "	C&CC

Army Form C. 2118.

WAR DIARY
or
INTELLIGENCE SUMMARY
(Erase heading not required.)

Instructions regarding War Diaries and Intelligence Summaries are contained in F. S. Regs., Part II. and the Staff Manual respectively. Title pages will be prepared in manuscript.

Place	Date	Hour	Summary of Events and Information	Remarks and references to Appendices
LES BREBIS.	10 "		2ND LT A.J.K DAVIS wounded in return. Bullet in wrist, accompanied by 1 O.R. as escort to Hospital.	C&CG
"	11		1 O.R. admitted to Hospital.	
"	12		1 O.R. discharged from Hospital.	C&CG
"			1 O.R. admitted to Hospital.	
"			1 O.R. (M.A.C.) joined company with 1 G.S. wagon and 2 R. fd. W. horses from No. 2 A.S.C Section A.H.T.D	
"	13		Relief between sections carried out. (S.O. No 12 attached)	
"	14		N.C.O. + 3 men proceeded to join the Br.Br.Q.C. (Heavies) for transfer/cavalry. D.A.G. 3rd Echelon. B.R. No 36607 a 7/11/16.	
"			1 O.R. reported from hospital where he had proceeded as escort to 2 Lt A.J.K.D.DAVIS.	
"	15		LIEUT MILLER E.B. proceed to leave to U.K to 2 Ha..a unit	C&CG
"	16		1 O.R. discharged from hospital.	
"	17		1 O.R. admitted to the hospital.	C&CG
			1 O.R. " " " "	C&CG

WAR DIARY
or
INTELLIGENCE SUMMARY.
(Erase heading not required.)

Army Form C. 2118.

Place	Date	Hour	Summary of Events and Information	Remarks and references to Appendices
LES BREBIS	19		1 O.R. admitted to Hospital.	C.O.R.G.
"	21		50 additional men fitted with new Box Respirators	
"	23		Leave in billets returned 200 teams in the line (C.O. N.º 13 attached)	
"	24		2nd Lt. F.A. PHILPOTT 1 Sergeant and 1 O.R returned from Br. Gen. School Camiers	
"	25		1 O.R. admitted to Hospital.	
"	"		2 O.R. granted leave to the United Kingdom to 6th December.	C.E.R.G.
"	26		2500 rounds fired on to Loos-Lens Road. Great difficulty in getting guns started, owing to thick lubricating oil.	C.E.R.G.
"	27		2nd Lt. W.M. WHITWORTH, 1 Sergeant + 1 O.R. sent on a course to Camiers (R.G.S. Lt. F.E.R. MILLER ordered to report to N.º 10th Hy Field Cy. R.E. Southy Subles	
"			No. a/538/2 d/- 25/11/16.	
"	28		1 O.R. discharged from Hospital.	
"	28		2nd Lts. LEFROY, J.E. FORSDIKE and J.T. SHILLITO joined Company from Reserve Gun Corps Base.	C.E.R.G.
"	29		Five sections teams from Billets relieved full teams in the line (as per Operation Order No. 14 attached) New "T" Very light Pistols issued sent up to the trenches	C.C.O.R.G.

Army Form C. 2118.

WAR DIARY
or
INTELLIGENCE SUMMARY.
(Erase heading not required.)

Instructions regarding War Diaries and Intelligence Summaries are contained in F. S. Regs., Part II. and the Staff Manual respectively. Title pages will be prepared in manuscript.

Place	Date	Hour	Summary of Events and Information	Remarks and references to Appendices
LES AREBIS	30		Two new Officers (2nd Lt. J.E. FORSKIKE, 2. Lt. J.T. SHILLITO) sent into the fire	CRC
			C.E. Cooper Lt for Major	
			O.C. 173rd Machine Gun Coy	

T2134. Wt. W708—776. 500000. 4/15. Sir J. C. & S.

SECRET
Ref.Sheet
36.B.1/40,000.   73rd MACHINE GUN COMPANY   Copy No......

OPERATION ORDER No. 11

Nov. 4th 1916.

1. The following team reliefs will take place in the line, during afternoon and evening, November 5th:-

    2 teams of No.1 Section releive teams in R.32 and R.33, which then return to billet.
    2 teams of No.3 Section releive teams in R.23,R.25, which then releive teams in S.11,S.12,which then return to billet.
    2 teams of No.4 Section releive teams in R.28,R.29, which releive teams in S.14,S.15,which then return to billet.
    1 team of No.2 Section releives team in R.27, which then releives team in S.13 which returns to billet.

2. In order to ensure that sections keep their own gun equipment the following will be adhered to:-
    Teams going from rear positions to forward positions will take with them their own gun equipment, viz., gun, spare parts, cleaning rod and spare barrel.

    Team returning from S.11 dumps gun eqpt at R.28 for incn. team
        "   "   " S.12   "   "   " " R.23 "   "   "
        "   "   " S.13   "   "   " " R.25 "   "   "
        "   "   " S.14   "   "   " " R.27 "   "   "
        "   "   " S.15 brings gun eqpt back to billet.

    Gun equipment for No.1 Section guns will not be changed.
    The No.4 Section team going into R.29 must take up gun equipment with it.

3. All other equipment not mentioned in para. 2 will be regarded as trench stores.

4. Lists of trench stores taken over by incoming N.C.O's will be sent in to Company Headquarters with 1st daily report.

5. Lt.Miller will releive 2/LT.Scott i/c R.30, R.31, R.32, R.33.
   2/Lt. Andrews "   "   Philpott" R.27,R.28,R.29,S.14,S.15.
   " Tibbitt "   "   Whitworth" R.23,R.25,S.11,S.12,S.13.

6. Officers will carefully hand over work in progress & proposed.

7. Teams will leave Company Headquarters under officers concerned at 2 p.m., November 5th.
    Handing over by N.C.O's must be thorough. Particular attention must be paid to ration and water arrangements. Officers must arrange that gun equipment is dealt with as in para., 2.
    Outgoing teams report to C.S.M. in their own time.

Sheet 2

8. Ration arrangements for night of November 5th and
onwards as usual.   Outgoing teams must carefully acquaint
incoming teams with arrangements re knots for rations.

9. Completion of releifs will be reported by Lt. Miller
and 2/Lt. Andrews to 2/Lt. Tippett, who will report company
releif complete by wiring the word "ORANGE".

Issued at 5.30 p.m.
Nov, 4th 1916.

                                        (sd) H.Gilbert, Major

                    Commanding 73rd Company, Machine Gun Corps.

War Diary

Secret 73rd Machine Gun Company. Copy No. 3
Ref Sheet
36.B.1/40,000 OPERATION ORDER No. 12

1. The following team reliefs will take place in the line during afternoon of November 13th:-

   2 teams of No.1 Section will relieve teams in R.30 and R.31, which then return to billets.
   2 teams in No.2 Section will relieve teams in R.27 and R.28, which will relieve S.13 and S.14, which then return to billets.
   2 teams in No.3 Section will relieve teams in R.23 and R.25, which will relieve S.11 and S.12, which then return to billets.
   1 team of No. 4 Section will relieve team in R.29, which will relieve S.15, which then returns to billet.
   1 team of No. 4 Section relieves team in F.1, which returns to billet.

2. In order to ensure that sections keep their own Gun Equipment, the following will be adhered to:-
   Teams going from rear positions to forward positions will take with them their own gun equipment, viz., gun, spare parts, cleaning rod, spare barrel and oil case.
   Team returning from S.11 dumps gun eqpt at R.23 for incn team
   "   "   "   S.12 "   "   "   " R.25 "   "   "
   "   "   "   S.13 "   "   "   " R.27 "   "   "
   "   "   "   S.14 "   "   "   " R.28 "   "   "
   "   "   "   S.15 "   "   "   " R.29 "   "   "

3. All gun equipment other than mentioned in Para.2 will be regarded as trench stores.

4. Lists of trench stores taken over by N.C.O's of incoming teams will be forwarded to Company Headquarters with the first daily report.

5. 2/Lt. Whitworth will relieve 2/Lt. Tibbitt i/c S.11, S.12, S.13, R.23, R.25.
   2/Lt. Scott will relieve Lt.Miller i/c R.30, R.31, R.32, R.33.

6. Officers will carefully hand over all work in progress and proposed.

7. Teams will leave Company Headquarters at 1.0 p.m. November 13th. Teams of No. 3 and 4 Sections will be marched off by 2/Lt. Whitworth.
   Teams of No.2 Section will be marched off by Sgt.Disney.

8. Handing over by N.C.O's must be thorough. Particular attention must be paid to Ration and Water arrangements.
   Teams will march out independently and will report to C.S.M. on their arrival at billets.

9. Officers will make their own arrangements about guides.

10. Horses for officers will be at "The Hole in the Wall" by 4.30 p.m.

(signed) H.Gilbert, Major.
Commanding 73rd Machine Gun Company.

Copy No.1 Brigade
  "   " 2 War Diary
  "   " 3   "   "
  "   " 4   "   "   Copy No.7 2/Lt.Andrews
                          "   " 8 "   Tibbitt
                          "   " 9 "   Whitworth
                          "   " 10 "   Scott
                          "   " 11 "   Bell
  "   " 5 File.   "   " 12 Sgt. Disney
  "   " 6 Lt. Miller

8.   The party at present working with 2/Lt.Tibbitt will proceed to their respective emplacements, and the following party will take their place:-

> L/C Morris
> Pte. Duce
> " Palmer
> " Windsor
> " Garratt
> " Hill
> " Kilborn
> " Horne.

9.   2/Lt.Andrews' working party will continue the present work they are on.

> (signed) H. Gilbert, Major.
> Commanding 73rd Machine Gun Company.

```
Copy No.1.... 73rd I.B.
 "   No.2.... War Diary.
 "   No.3....  "    "
 "   No.4....  "    "
 "   No.5.... File
 "   No.6.... Major Gilbert.
 "   No.7.... 2/Lt.Andrews.
 "   No.8.... 2/Lt.Scott.
 "   No.9.... 2/Lt.Tibbitt.
 "   No.10... 2/Lt.Whitworth.
 "   No.11... C.S.M.
 "   No.12... Officers Mess.
```

(1)

73rd MACHINE GUN COMPANY

Copy No. 2

OPERATION ORDER NO. 13.

1. The following team reliefs will take place in the line during afternoon of November 21st:-

   Sgt. Evans)
   Pte. Jackaman) Will relieve team in R.30, which will relieve
   " Main) S.14, which will return to billets.
   " Thomas)

   L/C Findley)
   Pte. Smyth) Will relieve team in R.31, which will relieve
   " Mudge) S.15, which will return to billets.
   " Maycock)

   Cpl. Dunkley)
   Pte. Murphy) Will relieve R.27, which will relieve S.11.
   " Hall) which will return to billets.
   " Wilson)

   Cpl. Batchelor)
   Pte. Paul) Will relieve R.28, which will relieve S.12,
   " Lockhart) which will return to billets.
   " Else)
   " Clay)

   Cpl. Mahon)
   Pte. Lawrence) Will relieve R.29, which will relieve S.13,
   " Lenehan) which will return to billets.
   " Rider)
   " Galley)

   Pte. Morris)
   " Shankland) Will relieve F.1, which will return to billets.
   " Poole)
   " Lindow)
   " Stocker)

2. All guns and equipment will be kept in their positions and handed over to the incoming team and attached to trench stores.

3. Lists of trench stores taken over by N.C.O's of incoming teams will be forwarded to Coy. Headquarters by first daily report.

4. The officers in the line will remain in their present positions and take charge of incoming teams and carry on with work in progress

5. Relieving teams will march off from Coy. Headquarters at 1.0.p.m. 21st November under their respective N.C.O's or senior privates.

6. Handing over by N.C.O's must be thorough.
   Teams will march out independently and report to C.S.M. directly they arrive in billets.

7. Officers will make their own arrangements about guides.

SECRET **73rd MACHINE GUN COMPANY.** No. 3
Ref. Sheet
56.B/M.GCC. OPERATION ORDER No.14

1. The following team reliefs will take place in the line during afternoon of Nov. 5.

   Sgt. Duithby)
   L/C Follows) Relieve R.32
   Pte Clayton)
   " Farish)

   Cpl. Plummer)
   Pte Watkins) Relieve R.35
   " Janes)
   " Lynch)

   Cpl. Dare)
   Pte Raven) Relieve S.14
   " Wilson)
   " Woolner)
   " Pearse)

   Sgt. Todd)
   Pte. Hodgkinson) Relieve S.11
   " Woodland)
   " Bayliss)
   " Pendlebury.

   L/C Fox)
   Pte Rayner)
   " Gradidge) Relieve S.15
   " Incles)
   " Nash)

   R.28 relieves S.12.   S.12 relieves R.28
   R.29 & Pte Hills from billet relieves F.1.   F.1   "   R.29

2. R.32, R.35, S.11, S.14, and S.15 on relief will march out independently and will report to C.S.M. on their arrival in billets.
   R.28 will proceed forward at 2.p.m. to relieve S.12, leaving 1 man behind to hand over R.28, after which he will rejoin his team.
   R.29 will proceed forward at 1.p.m. to relieve F.1, leaving 1 man behind to hand over R.29.

3. Teams will leave Company Headquarters at 1.p.m. November 5th under Sgt. Todd.

4. Lists of Trench Stores taken over by N.C.O's of incoming teams will be forwarded to Company Headquarters with the first Daily Report.

5. N.C.O's i/c teams will carefully hand over all work in progress and proposed.

6. All guns and gun equipment will remain in same emplacements and will be handed over as Trench Stores.

Issued at 8.30 p.m.   (signed) H. Gilbert, Major.
Nov. 30th 1916.   Commanding 73rd Machine Gun Company.

       Copy No.1 Brigade   Copy No.7 2/Lt. Tibbitt
            No.2 War Diary   8 "   Andrews
            No.3   "   "   9 "   Scott
            No.4   "   "   10 Sgt. Disney
            No.5 File   11 C.S.M.
            No.6 Major Gilbert   12 Officers Mess.

73rd Brigade.
24th Division.

73rd MACHINE GUN COMPANY.

DECEMBER 1 9 1 6.

Army Form C. 2118.

WAR DIARY
or
INTELLIGENCE SUMMARY.

(Erase heading not required.)

T332

July

Place	Date	Hour	Summary of Events and Information	Remarks and references to Appendices
Confidential			War Diary of Brigade Headquarters for the month of December 1916.	

WAR DIARY
or
INTELLIGENCE SUMMARY

(Erase heading not required.)

Army Form C. 2118.

Place	Date	Hour	Summary of Events and Information	Remarks and references to Appendices
LES BREBIS	1/1/16		MAJOR GILBERT admitted to hospital	Appx 2
			1 O.R. wounded in action	
	2		33 O.R's transferred to M.G.C on increase of establishment dating from 24/1/16 (Auth. D.A.G.C.R No. 16530/632a of 24/11 and Army Order 204/16	Appx 2
			1 O.R. admitted to hospital	Appx 2
	3		On night of the 3rd/4th the reconnaissance dumps were fired upon at intervals during the night. Reconnaissance fired 4,000.	Appx 2
	4		On the night of the 4/5th the enemy attempted a raid on our trenches opposite No 2 Lemmler Regt (for purposes of identification they entered our trenches at one place but failed to take a prisoner. One of our guns in the front line fired 1000 rounds, the result not known.	Appx 2
	5		Sric teams from bttals relieved sric teams in the line for 9 hrs. Operation Order No.15 attached)	Appx 2
	6		1 O.R admitted to hospital.	Appx 2
			4 O.R's reinforcements from Base Depot	Appx 2

WAR DIARY or INTELLIGENCE SUMMARY

Army Form C. 2118.

Place	Date	Hour	Summary of Events and Information	Remarks and references to Appendices
LA BREBIS	7		On the night of the 7/8th the roads and emplacements by the enemy were fired upon at intervals during the night.	Appx 1
	8		On the night of the 8/9th two guns were posted for barrage work.	
			At 10 p.m. 9 of our guns in cooperation with Stokes mortars carried out a combined shoot.	Appx 1 / 2 Appx 2
	9		1 O.R. admitted from hospital	
	10		On the night of the 10/11th 5 of our guns fired on gaps in enemy's wire and front line, made by a combined artillery and T.M. shoot during the day	2 Appx 2 / 2 Appx 2
	11		1 O.R. reinforcement from Base Depôt	
			2/Lieut. A.H. Wood struck off strength of Company from 3/9/15 (under C.R.O. 194 dated 10/12/15) for duty Defence by M.G. Barrage	2 Appx 1 / 2 Appx 1
	12		Tested 3 guns	
	13		1 O.R. admitted to hospital	
	14		1 O.R. sent to W.R.	
			3 O.R. wounded in action	Appx 1

Army Form C. 2118.

WAR DIARY
or
INTELLIGENCE SUMMARY.
(Erase heading not required.)

Place	Date	Hour	Summary of Events and Information	Remarks and references to Appendices
Les Angles	14.		On the morning the 11th S. teams from Regts relieved S. teams on the line Regt B.O. Nulle a C)	Appx L
	15.		1 O.Q. leave to U.K.	2 Appx L
	16.		1 O.R. leave to U.K. Our Vickers guns did a combined shoot on to ration roads and dumps used by the enemy.	2 Appx L
	17.		S. Teams from Btts relieved S. teams in the line (Ref att O.O. No.17).	2 Appx L
	18.		1 O.R. granted leave to U.K. 2/Lieut WHITWORTH and 2 O.R's returnees from School of Instruction Camiers	2 Appx L
	19.		2 O.R's joined from Base Depôt	2 Appx L
	20.		As a Chervelle to a combined shoot by our Heavy Artillery owing the day; two of our Vickers guns were ordered on to damaged enemy communication trenches and kept up a steady fire all through the night of the 20th/21st.	2 Appx L

WAR DIARY
or
INTELLIGENCE SUMMARY.
(Erase heading not required.)

Army Form C. 2118.

Place	Date	Hour	Summary of Events and Information	Remarks and references to Appendices
Les Brebis	21st		2nd Lieut WHITWORTH granted leave to U.K.	Appx 1
			Over the night of 21st/22nd our Vickers guns again fired on enemy trenches damaged by our artillery shoot of the previous day	Appx 2
	22		1 O.R. admitted to Hospital	
	23		1 O.R. granted leave to U.K.	
			5- Lewis gun teams relieved 5 teams in the line, in addition 2 men were attached to each of our 14 positions in the line of 191 Infy Bde Company for purposes of instruction. (Ref. O.O. No. 1F. att.)	Appx 1 Appx 2
	24		1 O.R. rejoined Company from Base Depot	
	25		On the night of the 25th/26th our Vickers guns carried out several shots in cooperation with artillery and French Mortars.	Appx 1
	26		1 O.R. admitted to Hospital	
			1 O.R. granted leave to U.K.	
			1 O.R. to No. 9 School Cameras for course of Instruction	Appx 1
	27		2nd Lieut T. BELL granted leave to U.K.	Appx 1
	28		1 O.R. discharged from Hospital	Appx 1

Army Form C. 2118.

WAR DIARY
or
INTELLIGENCE SUMMARY
(Erase heading not required.)

Instructions regarding War Diaries and Intelligence Summaries are contained in F.S. Regs., Part II and the Staff Manual respectively. Title pages will be prepared in manuscript.

Place	Date	Hour	Summary of Events and Information	Remarks and references to Appendices
LES BREBIS	28.		5 O.R.'s reinforcements joined from Base Depôt. All men of 191 at H.Q. Company attached to our teams in the line were withdrawn. 2nd Lieut J.H.D.BELL and 2nd Lieut E.M.TIBBITT promoted Lieutenant antedated 1/10/16.	Appx L
	29.		Major H. GILBERT discharged from hospital and rejoined the Company. 1 O.R. granted leave to U.K.	Appx L
	30.		5 teams from billets relieved 5 teams in the line. (Ref. O.O. No.20 att.) 1 O.R. granted leave to U.K.	Appx L
	31.		At 5 p.m. a test gas alarm was practised on the whole Brigade front. 1 O.R. granted leave to U.K.	Appx L Appx L

R. Watt Chaytor
O.C. 73 M.G. Company

SECRET
Ref Sheet
36B. 1/40000

73rd MACHINE GUN COMPANY

Copy No 2

OPERATION ORDER No. 15.

1. The following team reliefs will take place in the line during the afternoon of December 5th:-

    Cpl. Plummer   )
    Pte. Tunmore   )   Relieve F.1. F.1 relieve R.32. R.32
    " Robertson)   relieve S.13 R.23. R.23 return to
    " Shankland)   billets.
    " Douglas   )

    Sgt. Hubbard   )
    Pte. Buss   )   Relieve S.11. S.11 relieve R.33. R.33
    " Sylvester)   relieve S.13. S.13 return to billets.
    " Usherwood)
    " Bayliss   )

    L/C. March   )
    Pte. Staniforth)   Relieve S.12. S.12 return to billets.
    " Reid   )
    " Adams   )
    " Evans   )

    Sgt. Gregson   )
    Pte. Manton   )   Relieve S.14. S.14 relieve R.28. R.28
    " Curran   )   return to billets.
    " Murphy   )
    " Hills   )

    Pte. Patching   )
    " Swarbrick)   Relieve S.15. S.15 relieve R.25. R.25
    " Sargent   )   return to billets.
    " King   )
    " Murray   )

Pte. Hills from F.1. relieves Pte. Pearse S.14, who relieves Pte. Hall. R.27.

Pte. Incles from S.15 relieves Pte. Harness. R.27.

Ptes. Hall and Harness return to billets.

2. R.23, 25, 28, S.12, 13, Ptes. Hall and Harness on relief will march out independently and will report to C.S.M. on their arrival in billets.

3. Teams will leave Company Headquarters at 1.p.m. December 5th., under Sgt. Hubbard.

4. Lists of trench stores etc., taken over by N.C.O's of incoming teams will be forwarded to Company Headquarters with the first daily report.

                                                                  Contd. on next pag

Operation Order No.15. contd.

5. N.C.O's i/c teams will carefully hand over all work in progress and proposed.

6. 2/Lt.Scott will hand over all work in progress and proposed to 2/Lt.Shillito and return to billets.

Issued at 4.P.M.
3/12/16

                    (signed) C.E.R. Croager, Lt.
        Commanding 73rd Machine Gun Company.

```
Copy No. 1   73rd I.B.
         2   War Diary
         3    "    "
         4    "    "
         5   File
         6   Lt. Croager
         7   2/Lt. Tibbitt
         8    "   Philpott
         9    "   Andrews
        10    "   Scott
        11    "   Forsdike
        12    "   Shillito
        13   C.S.M.
        14   Sgt. Hubbard
        15   Officers Mess.
```

War Diary

SECRET
Ref
Sheet
36B 1/40000

Copy No...3...

73rd MACHINE GUN COMPANY.

OPERATION ORDER NO.16.

1. The following team reliefs will take place in the line during afternoon of December 11th:-

          (No.1 Team relieve F.1. F.1 relieve R.29. R.29 return to billets.
   No.2 (No.2 Team   "   S.11. S.11   "   R.30. R.30   "   "   "
   Setn (No.3 Team   "   S.12. S.12   "   R.31. R.31   "   "   "
          (No.4 Team   "   S.14. S.14   "   R.32. R.32   "   "   "
          (No.5 Team   "   S.15. S.15   "   R.33. R.33   "   "   "

   (See attached list of teams).

2. R.29 to R.33 on relief will march out independently and will report to C.S.M. on arrival in billets.

3. Teams will leave Company Headquarters at 1.p.m. December 11th, under Sgt.Raithby.

4. Lists of Trench Stores taken over by N.C.O's of incoming teams will be forwarded to Company Headquarters with the first daily report.

5. N.C.O's i/c of teams will carefully hand over all work in progress and proposed.

6. All guns and equipment will remain in same emplacements and will be handed over as trench stores.

                            (sgd) C.E.R. Croager. Lt.
             Commanding 73rd Machine Gun Company.

           Copy No.1   73rd I.B.
                2   War Diary
                3   "   "
                4   "   "
                5   File
                6   Major Gilbert
                7   Lt. Croager.
                8   2/Lt.Tibbitt.
                9   "   Philpott
             10   "   Andrews
             11   "   Scott
             12   "   Forsdike
             13   "   Shillito
             14   C.S.M.
             15   Sgt.Hubbard
             16   "   Raithby
             17   "   Todd
             18   "   Evans
             19   Officers Mess.

POSITIONS OF TEAMS BY SECTIONS WHEN RELIEF HAS BEEN COMPLETED.

No.1 SECTION.

No.1 Team.	R.29.	Cpl.Plummer, Shankland Maycock and Douglas.
No.2 Team.	R.30.	Sgt.Hubbard, Buss, Silvester, Usherwood.
No.3 Team.	R.31.	L/C March, Staniforth, Reid and Adams.
No.4 Team.	R.32.	Sgt.Gregson, Manton. Curran and Smyth.
No.5 Team.	R.33.	L/C Findley, Swarbrick Sargent and Patching.
In Billets.		Morris, Poole, Jackman, Main and Thomas.

No.2 SECTION.

No.1 Team.	F.1.	Sgt.Raithby, Campbell, Cooper, Farish and Jones.
No.2 Team.	S.11.	Cpl.Dunkley, Wks Evans, Hall, Clayton and Harness.
No.3 Team.	S.12.	L/C Follows, Paull, King, Lockhart and Murphy.
No.4 Team.	S.14.	Cpl.Batchelor, Lindow, Robertson, Stocker and Hills.
No.5 Team.	S.15.	Sgt.Disney, Tunmore, Else, Murray and Clay.
In billets.		Pte. Wilson.

No.3 SECTION.

No.1 Team.	In billets.	Sgt.Todd, Hodgkinson, Denman, Bayliss.
No.2 Team.	" "	Cpl.Clements, Batley, Rayner, Bell.
No.3 Team.	" "	L/C Davies, Elton, Wynn, Day.
No.4 Team.	" "	Sgt.Shorter, Mitchell, Bulley.
No.5 Team.	" "	Cpl.Mahon, Forrest, Fraser, Rider.

Working Party. In line. L/C Morris, Duce, Palmer, Windsor, Garrett, Kilborn Horne.

No.4 Section.

No.1 Team.	R.27.	Sgt.Evans, Galley, Ingles, Pearse.
No.2 Team.	R.28.	L/C Gardner, Seymour, Pudsey, Scally.
No.3 Team.	S.13.	Watkins, Jones, Lynch, Flanagan.
No.4 Team.	R.26.	Cpl.Dare, Raven, Wilson, Woolner.
No.5 Team.	R.25.	L/C Fox, Rayner, Gradidge, Nash.
In Billets.		Sgt.Searson, L/C Wolstenholme, Addis, Lawrence.

Working Party. In line. Cpl.Eeles, Lee, Kelly, Doughty, Riley, Mottram Rutherford.

SECRET
Ref
Sheet
36B 1/40000

Copy No 3.

73rd MACHINE GUN COMPANY

OPERATION ORDER NO. 17.

1. The following team reliefs will take place in the line during afternoon of December 17th:-

   Sgt. Todd)
   Pte. Hodgkinson)
   " Denman) Relieve F.1. F.1 relieve R.27. R.27 return
   " Bayliss) to billets. L/C. Bandey from billets will
   " Morris) relieve N.C.O. i/c team at R.27.

   Cpl. Clements)
   Pte. Batley)
   " Rayner) Relieve S.11. S.11 relieve S.13. S.13
   " Bell) return to billets.
   " Jackaman)

   L/C. Davies)
   Pte. Elton)
   " Wyman) Relieve S.12. S.12 relieve R.26. R.26
   " Day) return to billets.
   " Poole.)

   Sgt. Shorter)
   Pte. Mitchell)
   " Bulley) Relieve S.14. S.14 relieve R.25. R.25
   " Kimberley) return to billets.
   " Mudge)

   Cpl. Mahon)
   Pte. Forrest)
   " Fraser) Relieve S.15. S.15 relieve R.23. R.23
   " Rider) return to billets.
   " Main)

2. On arrival of relieving teams at F.1, S.11, 12, 14 & 15, the undermentioned men will return to billets:-

   Ptes. Harness, Murphy, Hills, Addis, Thomas, Murray.

3. S.13, R.23, 25, 27, 28 and men detailed, on relief will march out independently and will report to C.S.M. on arrival in billets.

4. Teams will leave Company Headquarters at 1.p.m. December 17th under Sgt. Todd.

5. Lists of trench stores taken over by N.C.O's of incoming teams will be forwarded to Company Headquarters with the first daily report.

6. N.C.O's i/c of teams will carefully hand over all work in progress and proposed.

(contd. on next page)

7. All guns and equipment will remain in same emplacements and will be handed over as trench stores.

8. 2/Lt.Andrews will relieve 2/Lt.Shillito, who will then relieve 2/Lt.Philpott at R.23.
2/Lt.Whitworth will relieve 2/Lt.Forsdike at Centre Group.

          (sgd) C.E.R. Croager, Lt.
      Commanding 73rd Machine Gun Company.

Issued at 6.p.m.
December 15th 1916.

```
Copy No. 1  73rd I.B.
         2  War Diary
         3   "     "
         4   "     "
         5  File
         6  Major Gilbert
         7  Lt. Croager
         8  2/Lt. Tibbitt
         9    "   Philpott
        10    "   Whitworth
        11    "   Andrews
        12    "   Scott
        13    "   Forsdike
        14    "   Shillito
        15  C.S.M.
        16  Sgt. Disney
        17   "   Todd
        18   "   Evans
        19  Officers Mess.
```

SECRET
Ref
Sheet
56B.1/40000

73rd MACHINE GUN COMPANY

Copy No. 5

OPERATION ORDER No. 18.

1. The following team reliefs will take place in the line during afternoon of December 23rd:-

    Cpl. Dare
    Pte. Woolner
    " Flanagan
    Two men of
    191st Coy.
    } Relieve S.11. S.11 relieve R.29. R.29 return to billets.

    L/C. Fox
    Pte. Seymour
    " Scally
    Two men of
    191st Coy.
    } Relieve S.12. S.12 relieve R.30. R.30 return to billets.

    L/C. Wolstenholme
    Pte. Watkins
    " James
    Two men of
    191st Coy.
    } Relieve S.14. S.14 relieve R.31. R.31 return to billets.

    Sgt. Evans
    Pte. Wilson
    " Galley
    Two men of
    191st Coy.
    } Relieve S.15. S.15 relieve R.32. R.32 return to billets.

    Sgt. Todd
    Pte. Hodgkinson
    " Denman
    Two men of
    191st Coy.
    } Relieve R.33. R.33 return to billets.

2. Two men will be detailed by 191st Machine Gun Company to report to each of the following positions:-
    S.13, R.23, R.25, R.27, R.28, R.29, R.30, R.31, and R.32.
On arrival of these men the undermentioned men will return to billets:-
    Ptes. Bell, Day, Kimberley, Jackaman, Poole, Mudge, Main, Wilson, King, Robertson, Evans, and Tunmore.

3. R.28, R.30, R.31, R.32, R.33 and men detailed, on relief will march out independently and will report to C.S.M. on arrival in billets.

4. Teams will leave Company Headquarters at 1.p.m. December 23rd under 2/Lt. Philpott.

5. Lists of Trench Stores taken over by N.C.O's of incoming teams will be forwarded to Company Headquarters with the first Daily Report.

(contd. on next page)

"War Diary"

6. Officers, and N.C.O's i/c of teams will carefully hand over all work in progress and proposed.

7. 2/Lt.Forsdike will relieve 2/Lt.Shillito in Right Group.
2/Lt.Philpott will relieve 2/Lt.Scott in Centre Group.

8. Working parties under Cpl.Eeles and L/Cpl.Morris will return to billets on evening of December 23rd and will report to C.S.M. on arrival.

(sgd) C.E.R. Croager, Lt.
Commanding 73rd Machine Gun Company.

Copy No.1	73rd I.B.	Copy No.10	2/Lt.Philpott
2	191st M.G. Coy.	11	" Andrews
3	War Diary	12	" Scott
4	War Diary	13	" Forsdike
5	War Diary	14	" Shillito
6	File	15	C.S.M.
7	Major Gilbert	16	Sgt. Evans
8	Lt. Croager.	17	" Hubbard
9	2/Lt. Tibbitt.	18	" Shorter

Copy No.19. Officers Mess.

SECRET.
Ref
Sheet
36B. 1/40000

73rd MACHINE GUN COMPANY

OPERATION ORDER NO. 19.

Copy No...4....

1.   The following team reliefs will take place in the line during afternoon of December 29th:-

Sgt. Hubbard, Ptes. Buss and Usherwood relieve S.14. S.14 relieve R.27. R.27 return to billets.

L/C. March, Ptes. Reid and Staniforth relieve S.15. S.15 relieve R.28. R.28 return to billets.

Cpl. Plummer, Ptes. Shankland and Douglas relieve S.13. S.13 return to billets.

Ptes. Manton, Sylvester and Sargent relieve R.30. R.30 return to billets.

Sgt. Gregson, Ptes. Smyth and Adams relieve R.32. R.32 return to billets.

Cpl. Smith, Ptes. Thomas and Mudge relieve R.29. R.29 return to billets.

Ptes. Patching, Swarbrick and Morris relieve R.31. R.31 return to billets.

Ptes. Pudsey, Nash and Lynch relieve R.33. R.33 return to billets.

Ptes. Doughty, Raven and Addis relieve R.23. R.23 return to billets.

Ptes. Poole, Main and King relieve R.25. R.25 return to billets.

2.   O.C. 191st M.G. Company will detail 2 men to report to each of the following positions:-
        S.11, 12, 13, 14, 15, R.23, 25, 27, 28, 29, 30, 31, 32 & 33.

3.   On relief all teams will march out independently and report to C.S.M. on arrival in billets.
        N.C.O's and men of 191 Coy will return to their own billets, reporting on arrival.

4.   Teams will leave Company Headquarters at 1.p.m. December 29th, under 2/Lt. Scott.

5.   Lists of trench stores taken over by N.C.O's of incoming teams will be forwarded to Company Headquarters with the first daily report.

6.   N.C.O's i/c teams will carefully hand over all work in progress and proposed.

(continued on next page)

page 2.

7. All guns and equipment will remain in ~~same emplacements~~
   and ~~will be handed~~ over as trench stores.

8. 2/Lt. Scott will relieve 2/Lt. Andrews,
   " Shillito will supervise working parties in Centre
   Group.

9. Working parties under Cpl. Eeles and L/Cpl. Morris will
   return to the trenches with the relieving teams.

                        (sgd) C.E.R. Croager. Lt.
           Commanding 73rd Machine Gun Company.

Issued at 8.p.m.
December 27th 1916.

```
Copy No. 1   73rd I.B.
         2   191st M.G. Coy.
         3   War Diary
         4     "     "
         5     "     "
         6   File
         7   Major Gilbert.
         8   Lt. Croager.
         9   2/Lt. Tibbitt.
        10    "   Philpott.
        11    "   Andrews.
        12    "   Scott.
        13    "   Forsdike.
        14    "   Shillito.
        15    "   C.S.M.
        16   Sgt. Hubbard.
        17    "   Disney.
        18    "   Todd.
        19.   "   Evans
        20   Officers Mess.
```

War Diary

SECRET
Ref
Sheet
36B. 1/40000.

73rd MACHINE GUN COMPANY

OPERATION ORDER NO. 20.

Copy No. 3

1.   Operation Order No.19 dated 27/12/16 is hereby cancelled, and the following substituted.

2.   The following team reliefs will take place in the line during afternoon of December 29th:-

    Sgt. Gregson   )
    Pte. Manton   )
    " Smyth   ) Relieve S.11. S.11 relieve R.23. R.23
    " Poole   ) return to billets.
    " Jackaman   )

    Cpl. Smith   )
    Pte. Patching   ) Relieve S.12. S.12 relieve R.25. R.25
    " Swarbrick   ) return to billets.
    " Sargent   )
    " Thomas   )

    Cpl. Plummer   )
    Pte. Shankland   ) Relieve S.13. S.13 return to billets.
    " Morris   )
    " Douglas   (

    Sgt. Hubbard   )
    Pte. Buss   ) Relieve S.14. S.14 relieve R.27. R.27
    " Sylvester   ) return to billets.
    " Usherwood   )
    " Rider   )

    L/C. March   )
    Pte. Staniforth   ) Relieve S.15. S.15 relieve R.28. R.28
    " Reid   ) return to billets.
    " Adams   )
    " Mudge   )

3.   On arrival of relieving teams at S.11, 12, 13, 14 & 15, R.23, 25, 27 & 28, the undermentioned men return to billets:-

    Ptes. Jones, Evans, Wilson, Hall and Tunmore.

    The following will remain with the relieving team:-

    Ptes. Lynch, Raven, Doughty and Gradidge.

4.   On relief, all teams and men detailed will march out independently and will report to C.S.M. on arrival in billets.

5.   Teams will leave Company Headquarters at 1.p.m. December 29th, under Sgt. Hubbard.

6.   Lists of trench stores taken over by N.C.O's of incoming teams will be forwarded to Company Headquarters with the first daily report.

(contd. on next page)

7. N.C.O's i/c of teams will carefully hand over all work in progress and proposed.

8. All guns and equipment will remain in same emplacements and will be handed over as trench stores.

9. 2/Lt. Scott will relieve 2/Lt. Andrews.

   " Shillito will supervise working parties in Centre Group.

10. Working parties under Cpl. Eeles and L/Cpl. Morris will return to the trenches with the relieving teams.

                              (sgd) C.E.R. Croager, Lt.
                Commanding 73rd Machine Gun Company

Issued at 6.p.m.
December 28th 1916.

                Copy No. 1 73rd I.B.
                       2 War Diary
                       3 "   "
                       4 "   "
                       5 File
                       6 Major Gilbert
                       7 Lt. Croager
                       8 2/Lt. Tibbitt
                       9 "   Philpott
                     10 "   Andrews
                     11 "   Scott
                     12 "   Forsdike
                     13 "   Shillito
                     14 C.S.M.
                     15 Sgt. Hubbard
                     16 " Disney
                     17 " Todd
                     18 " Evans
                     19 Officers Mess.

Army Form C. 2118.

WAR DIARY
or
INTELLIGENCE SUMMARY.
(Erase heading not required.)

Instructions regarding War Diaries and Intelligence
Summaries are contained in F. S. Regs., Part II.
and the Staff Manual respectively. Title pages
will be prepared in manuscript.

Place	Date	Hour	Summary of Events and Information	Remarks and references to Appendices

Vol 10

War Diary of
4th Machine Gun Company
for the month of
January 1917

WAR DIARY
or
INTELLIGENCE SUMMARY.
(Erase heading not required.)

Army Form C. 2118.

Instructions regarding War Diaries and Intelligence Summaries are contained in F. S. Regs., Part II. and the Staff Manual respectively. Title pages will be prepared in manuscript.

Place	Date	Hour	Summary of Events and Information	Remarks and references to Appendices
LES BREBIS.	1st Jan '17		3 O.Rank sent to Divisional L.G. School on a course of Signalling at BRAQUEMONT. 6616 Sgt Hubbard J.F. awarded D.C.M (as per London Gazette of that date)	C.E.G.
"	2nd		1 O.R. admitted to Hospital. 2nd Lt WILD W.P. and 30 O.R. attached to the Company from the 1st Cavalry Machine Gun Squadron.	C.E.G.
"	3		5000 rounds fired at enemy's dumps & much trouble experienced with fuses. Blindages reported of fired. SAA. Team relief took place during afternoon, four of our teams being relieved by four teams consisting of 27 O.R. of the 1st C.M.G. Squadron (Operation Order No 21 attached)	C.E.G.
"	4		5000 rounds fired at enemy communication trenches. 1 Ordinary Rank admitted to Hospital	C.E.G.
"	6			
"	7		Two guns ordered by Division through Brigade to be stationed at L.3 and 6.6. (Sheet 36.b. N.42000.) to fire at enemy aircraft. 500 rounds consisting of 12 men 1 NCO + 1 officer. 1 O.R. admitted to Hospital.	C.E.G.
	8		4500 rounds fired during night of 7/8th at enemy dumps &c. 1 O.R. admitted to Hospital 1 O.R. granted leave to U.K. to the 16th Jan.	

WAR DIARY
or
INTELLIGENCE SUMMARY.
(Erase heading not required.)

Army Form C. 2118.

Place	Date	Hour	Summary of Events and Information	Remarks and references to Appendices
LESBKREBIS	6		8500 bombs fired at enemy communication trenches & dumps &c	C.B.G.
LESBREBIS.	9th		1 O.R. discharged from Hospital	C.B.G.
"	10		Enemy trenches raided by party of 2nd Kensa R Regt. Eight guns fired to support said. Total number of rounds fired 40,000. (Special order issued re attacks).	
			1 O.R. discharged from Hospital	
			1 O.R. wounded in action (Shrapnel in face)	
			Anti aircraft guns fired four belts (1000Rds) at hostile aeroplane during the night without apparent success.	
"	12		1 O.R. wounded in action (concussion & slight shrapnel)	
"	13		1 O.R. sent to No 1 Ordnance Mobile Workshop for 1 months course on probation as an Artificer	C.B.G.
"	12		Up to date 12.5 O.R. have been trained with new Revolver. Same relief took place in the line (operation order No 22 attached)	C.B.G.
"	13		2 O.R. returned to their unit the 15 Car. M.G. squadron.	C.B.G.
"	14		1 O.R. admitted to Hospital	
"	15		1 O.R. discharged from Hospital	C.B.G.
			Major GILBERT 30 days leave to U.K.	

Army Form C. 2118.

WAR DIARY
or
INTELLIGENCE SUMMARY.
(Erase heading not required.)

Instructions regarding War Diaries and Intelligence Summaries are contained in F. S. Regs., Part II. and the Staff Manual respectively. Title pages will be prepared in manuscript.

Place	Date	Hour	Summary of Events and Information	Remarks and references to Appendices
LES BRIEBIS	15.		1 O.R. discharged from hospital	
	16.		1 O.R. Leave to U.K.	
			1 O.R. returned to duty from leave at R.G. School Camiers	L/Cpl L
			2 O.R.'s wound in action	
			1 O.R. discharged from hospital	
			Our Vickers gun's burnt out a combined shot dump the night on ration roads and dumps used by the enemy	L/Cpl L
	17.		1 O.R. killed in action	Pte G
	18.		1 O.R. wounded in action	
			8 teams from billet relieved 8 teams in the line (Ref attached)	
			C. O. Chamber 23.	L/Cpl L
	19.		1 O.R. discharged from hospital.	T/Maj Y
	20.		1 O.R. Leave to U.K.	L/Cpl L
	21.		At 9.15 a.m. enemy lines were raided by a party of the 13th Churchill were Rifl. In support of this above of our guns fired in all 38,000 rounds in enemy's importance	

WAR DIARY or INTELLIGENCE SUMMARY

Army Form C. 2118.

(Erase heading not required.)

Instructions regarding War Diaries and Intelligence Summaries are contained in F. S. Regs., Part II. and the Staff Manual respectively. Title pages will be prepared in manuscript.

Place	Date	Hour	Summary of Events and Information	Remarks and references to Appendices
LES BREBIS	21		Communications trenches (Special Orders issued as attached).	EBL
	22		2/Lieut Walker of the 1st M.G. Squadron rejoins his unit to take up temporary command.	EBL
			1 O.R. wounded in action.	EBL
			2 O.R. admitted to hospital	EBL
	23		6 Vickers guns cooperate with the Artillery on a combined shoot on routes and tracks suspected to be used by the enemy for a relief.	EBL
	24		4 teams from Pullets relieve 4 teams in the line (Ref. attached) of Section Area No. 25.	EBL
	25		During the night of the 25th/26th our guns fires on a ten rounds and clumps used by the enemy.	EBL
	26		At 6.45 a.m. fire from guns fired on back area opposite the next Brigade front whilst a successful raid was carried out by them. In all our guns fired 25,000 rounds.	EBL
			2/Lieut P.H. 17077 and 1 O.R. proceeded to 1st Army A.A. Group for a Course	EBL

WAR DIARY
or
INTELLIGENCE SUMMARY

Army Form C. 2118.

Instructions regarding War Diaries and Intelligence Summaries are contained in F. S. Regs., Part II. and the Staff Manual respectively. Title pages will be prepared in manuscript.

(Erase heading not required.)

Place	Date	Hour	Summary of Events and Information	Remarks and references to Appendices
ES BREBIS	26th		Anti aircraft centre. 1 O.R. proceeded to U.K. to take up a commission. 1 O.R. discharged from hospital.	E.Ch.
	27th		The relief which was to take place on cable Durancourt Front cancelled.	E.Ch.
	28th		The 1st Cav. R. G. Squadron attached for duty. Proceeded near to Renin avec character.	E.Ch.
	29th		2 men attached to 12 of our gun position in the line from the 1st Cavalry R.G. Squadron. 2 guns mounted in back area for anti-aircraft enterprised on the occasion at hostile aeroplanes but without apparent avenir.	E.Ch.
	30th		12 people in the line were relieved by the 1st Cav. aby. R. G. Squadron of G.Rs. of the 1st R. G. Squadron returned to their unit.	E.Ch.
			1 O.R. admitted to hospital.	L.Ch.
	31st		1 O.R. discharged from hospital.	E.Ch.

Army Form C. 2118.

WAR DIARY
or
INTELLIGENCE SUMMARY.
(Erase heading not required.)

Instructions regarding War Diaries and Intelligence Summaries are contained in F. S. Regs., Part II. and the Staff Manual respectively. Title pages will be prepared in manuscript.

Place	Date	Hour	Summary of Events and Information	Remarks and references to Appendices
LES BREBIS	21st		1 OR. admitted to hospital. 2/Lieut WHITWORTH and 1 man left at escort of the 12 horses taken over by the 9 " Car. M. G. Squadron, returned to billets. Owing to a large percentage of the Company being in billets, a system of training commenced.	Sgd.

2/M. Tibbits Lieut.
for O.C. 73 M.G. Company

SECRET
Ref
Sheet
36B 1/40000

73rd MACHINE GUN COMPANY.

Copy No... 5 ....

OPERATION ORDER NO. 21.

1. The following team reliefs will take place on the afternoon and evening of 4th January:-

    Sgt. Raithby)
    Pte. Campbell) to relieve S.11, who will relieve R.23, who
    " Jones) return to billets.
    " Murphy)
    " Jackaman)

    Cpl. Dunkley)
    Pte. Wilson) to relieve S.13, who will relieve R.25, who
    " Hall) return to billets.
    " Clayton)
    " Thorpe)

    L/C. Follows)
    Pte. Paull) to relieve S.14, who will relieve R.27, who
    " Lockhart) return to billets.
    " Harness)
    " Incles)

    Sgt. Disney)
    Pte. Evans) to relieve S.15, who will relieve R.28, who
    " King) return to billets.
    " Rowland)
    " Mudge)

Pte. Thomas will return to billets from S.12 on being relieved.

2. The following reliefs will take place after dark by teams of the Cavalry Section, who will take into the line with them:-

                4 Guns.
                4 Gun cases.
                4 Spare parts cases.
                4 Oil cases.
                4 Cleaning rods.
                4 Spare barrels.

    Sgt. Shook)
    Cpl. Wiles)
    Pte. Brent) To relieve team at R.30, who will return
    " Withers) to billets.
    " Lipscombe)
    " Simmons)
    " Ayton)

    Sgt. Hubbard)
    Pte. Wrathell)
    " Davis) To relieve team at R.31, who will return
    " Guy) to billets.
    " Riseley)
    " Carter)
    " Isaacs)

(contd. on next page)

page 2.

2. (contd).   Cpl. Fogg)
              "   Eke   )
              Pte. Reeves)   to relieve R.32, who will return
              "   Linford)   to billets.
              "   Anderson)
              "   Cook   )
              "   Mell   )

              Cpl. Kertland)
              Pte. Corscaden)
              "   Ellis   )   to relieve R.33, who will return
              "   Bower   )   to billets.
              "   Taylor)
              "   Gamble)

3. The above teams will march off from Coy. Q.M. Stores at 4.30.p.m. for Hatchetts. 2/Lt. Scott will arrange for guides from R.30, 31, 32 & 33 to meet incoming cavalry teams at Hatchetts.

4. 2/Lt. Scott is held responsible for:-

   (a). Thorough handing over by present team N.C.O's to Cavalry N.C.O's, as the Cavalry Section is not acquainted with this part of the line.
   (b). That on relief all dugouts and emplacements are left in a thoroughly clean condition.
   (c). The following equipment belonging to this company will be brought out of the positions by each relieved team and packed in a waiting limber for return to Coy. H.Q.:-
        1 Gun
        1 Gun case
        1 Spare parts case
        1 Oil case
        1 Spare barrel
        1 Cleaning rod
   (d). Relieved teams will march out under the Senior N.C.O. and will report to C.S.M. on arrival at billets.

5. 2/Lt. Andrews will accompany 2/Lt. Wild at the Loos Enclosure. Sgt. Hubbard will accompany Sgt. Shook at the Loos Enclosure. Lt. Tibbitt will relieve 2/Lt. Shillito, who will relieve 2/Lt. Philpott, who returns to billets. 2/Lt. Whitworth will relieve 2/Lt. Forsdike at R.23.

6. Teams, except as mentioned in para 4 will be marched off from Company Headquarters at 1.0.p.m. by 2/Lt. Whitworth.

7. On relief, except teams as mentioned in para 4, teams will march off independently and report to C.S.M. on their arrival at billets.

8. Lists of trench stores taken over by N.C.O's of incoming teams will be forwarded to Company Headquarters with first daily report.

9. Officers in charge of groups will hand over very carefully all work in progress and proposed.

10. All guns and equipment will remain in same emplacements (except as mentioned in para 4) and will be handed over as trench stores.

P.T.O.

11. Working parties will remain in their present positions.

                                    (sgd) H. Gilbert, Major.
                      Commanding 73rd Machine Gun Company.

Issued at 6.p.m.
January 3rd 1916.

        Copy No. 1   73rd I.B.
                2   O.C. No.1 M.G. Squadron.
                3   War Diary
                4   "   "
                5   "   "
                6   File.
                7   Major Gilbert.
                8   Lt. Croager.
                9   " Tibbitt.
              10   2/Lt. Philpott.
              11   " Andrews.
              12   " Scott
              13   " Forsdike.
              14   " Shillito.
              15   " Wild.
              16   C.S.M.
              17   Sgt. Hubbard.
              18   " Shook.
              19   Officers Mess.

SECRET 73rd MACHINE GUN COMPANY. Copy No. 5
Ref sheet
56B 1/40000 OPERATION ORDER NO. 22.

1. The following team reliefs will take place in the line during afternoon of January 12th:-

   Sgt. Shorter   )   Cpl. Mahon   )
   Pte. Bayliss   ) Relieve S.11 who   Pte. Forrest) Relieve S.12 who
    "   Kimberley) relieve R.34 who   "   Fraser   ) relieve R.35 who
    "   Culshaw   ) return to billets.   "   Rider   ) return to billets.
    "   Pruce   )   "   Addis   )

   Cpl. Clements   )   L/C. Davies   )
   Pte. Rayner   ) Relieve S.13 who   Pte. Wyman   ) Relieve S.14 who
    "   Bell   ) return to billets.   "   Elton   ) return to billets.
    "   Lee   )   "   Roberts)
    "   Rutherford)   "   Main   )

   Sgt. Todd   )   Cpl. Dare   )
   Pte. Hodgkinson) Relieve S.15 who   Pte. Woolner) Relieve R.27 who
    "   Denman   ) return to billets.   "   Flanagan) return to billets.
    "   Dallimore)   "   Murray   )
    "   Curran   )

   L/C. Fox   )   Cpl. Eeles   )
   Pte. Galley   ) Relieve R.26 who   Pte. Lenehan) Relieve R.28 who
    "   Gradidge   ) return to billets.   "   Mottram) return to billets.
    "   Nash   )   "   Riley   )

   Ptes. Wardrobe and Raven will remain at R.34 position.
   Sgt. Evans will relieve Sgt. Hubbard at R.31.
   On arrival of the relieving teams at S.11 and S.12 Ptes. Jackaman and Thorpe will return to billets.

   The Cavalry Section at the ENCLOSURE will remain in their present positions.

2. 2/Lt. Scott will relieve 2/Lt. Shillito.

3. Teams will leave Company Headquarters at 1. p.m. January 12th, under 2/Lt. Scott.

4. On relief, teams returning to billets will march off independently and report their arrival to C.S.M. at Company Headquarters.

5. Lists of trench stores taken over by N.C.O's of incoming teams will be forwarded to Company Headquarters with first daily report.

6. Officers i/c of groups will hand over very carefully all work in progress and proposed.

7. All guns and equipment will remain in same emplacements and will be handed over as trench stores.

8. Working parties will remain in their present positions.

9. 2/LT. SHILLITO's horse will be at "The Hole in the Wall" at 4. p.m.

Issued at 8. p.m. 11/1/17.

(sgd) H. Gilbert, Major.
Commanding 73rd Machine Gun Company.

Copy No. 1 73rd I.B.   Copy No. 9 Lt. Tibbitt
         2 O.C. No.1 M.G. Squadron.   10 2/Lt. Scott
         3 War Diary   11   "   Shillito.
         4   "   "   12   "   Whitworth
         5   "   "   13 Lt. Wilde.
         6 File   14 Sgt. Hubbard.
         7 Major Gilbert   15 C.S.M.
         8 Lt. Croager.   16 Officers Mess.

War Diary

Copy No..........

1st Sheet
OOR X/4000

23rd MACHINE GUN COMPANY

OPERATION ORDER NO.25.

1. Operation Order No.25 dated January 13th is cancelled and the following substituted.

2. The following team reliefs will take place in the line during the afternoon of January 14th:-

Sgt.Evans)	L/Sgt.Clements)
Pte.Lee) Relieve F.A.	Pte.Bell) Relieve S.1a.S.4.
" Rutherford)	" Haycock) relieve R.37.C.37
" Raven)	" Ashton) return to billets
" Bayliss)	" Main)

Cpl.Bentley)	Sgt.Raithby)
Pte.Wilson) Relieve S.1a.S.4	Pte.Campbell) Relieve R.35.R.45
" Hall) relieve R.35.R.50	" Jones) return to billets
" Clayton) return to billets	" Murphy)
" Wardrobe)	

Pte.Hodgkinson, L.4. and L/C Findley, S.4a, on arrival of relieving teams will return to billets.

3. 2/Lt.Shillito will relieve 2/Lt.Philpott.
   2/Lt.Whitworth will relieve 2/Lt.Scott.

4. Teams will leave Company Headquarters at 4.p.m. on January 14th, under 2/Lt.Whitworth.

5. On relief, teams returning to billets will march out independently and will report to C.S.M. on arrival in billets.

6. Lists of Trench Stores taken over by N.C.O's of incoming teams will be forwarded to Company Headquarters with the first daily report.

7. Officers i/c of groups will hand over very carefully all work in progress and proposed.

8. All guns and equipment will remain as at present and will be handed over to incoming teams.

9. Working parties will remain in their present positions.

Issued at 12 noon
January 14th 1917.

(sgd) C.A... Crozier, Lt.
Commanding 23rd Machine Gun Company.

Copy No. 1 War I.D.   Copy No. 10 2/Lt.Whitworth
        2 No.4 M.G. Squadron   11   " Andrews.
        3 War Diary   12   " Scott.
        4   "   "   13   " Forsdike
        5   "   "   14   " Shillito
        6 File   15 Sgt. ...
        7 Lt.Crozier   16   " Dunn.
        8   " Tibbitt.   17 C.S.M.
        9 2/Lt.Philpott.   18 Officers Mess.

SECRET   73rd MACHINE GUN COMPANY   Copy No. 3
Ref Sheet
36B 1/40000   OPERATION ORDER No. 23.

1. The following team reliefs will take place in the line during afternoon of 18th January:-

   Sgt. Disney   )   Cpl. Batchelor)
   Pte. Evans   ) Relieve S.11.S.11   Pte. Lindow   ) Relieve S.12.S.12
   "   King   ) relieve R.25.R.25   "   Robertson) relieve R.24.R.24
   "   Rowland   ) return to billets   "   Stocker   ) return to billets
   "   Pruce   )   "   Murray   )

   L/C. Follows   )   L/C. Bandey   )
   Pte. Paull   ) Relieve S.13.S.13   Pte. Hodgkinson) Relieve S.14.S.14
   "   Lockhart   ) return to billets   "   Batley   ) return to billets
   "   Harness   )   "   Bulley   )
   "   Watkins   )   "   Kilborn   )

                  Sgt. Gregson)
                  L/C. Findley) Relieve S.15
                  Pte. Manton) S.15 return
                  "   Poole   ) to billets.
                  "   Smyth   )

   Pte. Pruce, S.11, to remain at S.11 with the relieving team.
   Pte. Doughty to relieve Pte. Raven at R.24.

2. The following team reliefs will take place in the line during the evening of January 18th:-

   Sgt. Hubbard   )   L/C. March   )
   Pte. Sylvester) Relieve R.30.R.30   Pte. Staniforth) Relieve R.31. R.31
   "   Usherwood   ) return to billets   "   Reid   ) return to billets
   "   Mudge   )   "   Thorpe   )

   Cpl. Plummer   )   Cpl. Smith   )
   Pte. Morris   ) Relieve R.32.R.32   Pte. Patching   ) Relieve R.33.R.33
   "   Jackaman   ) return to billets   "   Swarbrick   ) return to billets
   "   Douglas   )   "   Sargent   )

3. 2/Lt. Andrews will relieve 2/Lt. Whitworth at R.33.
   "   Forsdike   "   "   Lt. Wild in Loos Sector.

4. Teams proceeding to S.11, 12, 13, 14 & 15 will march off from Company Headquarters at 1.p.m. under 2/Lt. Andrews.
   Teams proceeding to R.30, 31, 32, & 33 will march off from Company Headquarters at 4.30.p.m. under 2/Lt. Forsdike & will proceed via MAROC to HATCHETTS, where they will await the gun limber.

5. The teams proceeding to R.30, 31, 32 & 33 will take with them on the limber:-

                  1 Gun
                  1 Gun case
                  1 Spare parts case
                  1 Oil case
                  1 Spare barrel
                  1 Cleaning rod

6. Teams mentioned in para 1 will on relief march out independently and will report to C.S.M. on their arrival in billets.

7. Teams mentioned in para 2 will on relief convey all equipment belonging to Cavalry Company to HATCHETTS, where it will be packed on the limber under the direction of Lt. Wild. When this is complete they will march back to Company Headquarters under the senior N.C.O. who will report to C.S.M. on arrival in billets.

8. Lists of trench stores taken over by N.C.O's of incoming teams will be forwarded to Coy. Headquarters with the first daily report.

(contd on next page)

War Dept

9. Officers in charge of groups will hand over very carefully all work in progress and proposed.

10. Working parties will remain in their present positions.

11. 1 Ammunition Limber to be at Company Billets at 4.p.m. to convey gun equipment to HATCHETTS.

Issued at 8.p.m.
January 16th 1917.

(sgd) H. Gilbert, Major. M.C.
Commanding 73rd Machine Gun Company.

Copy No. 1 73rd I.B.
       2 1st M.G. Squadron.
       3 War Diary.
       4 " "
       5 " "
       6 File
       7 Lt. Croager.
       8 " Tibbitt.
       9 " Bell.

Copy No. 10 Lt. Wild
       11 2/Lt. Philpott.
       12 " Whitworth.
       13 " Andrews.
       14 " Scott.
       15 " Forsdike.
       16 C.S.M.
       17 Sgt. Hubbard.
       18 " Disney.

Copy No. 19. Officers Mess.

73 Company Machine Gun Corps.   Copy No. 4

OPERATION ORDER NO. 26.

1. 12 guns of the 73rd M.Gun Coy will be relieved in the LOOS SECTION by the 9th Cav.M.G.Sqdrn on the 30th Jany.

2. The following guns will be relieved by the 9th Cav.M.Gun Sqdrn:- S.11. S.12. S.13.a. S.14. S.15. R.24. R.27. R.28. R.29. R.30. R.31. F.1 2 Teams from billets will relieve R.32 & R.33.

3. 2 men from the 9th Cav.M.Gun Sqdrn. will be attached to each of the 12 teams on the 29th and will stay at these positions until the remainder of their company arrive on the following day.

4. On the 30th Jany. the relieving teams will arrive at the Hole in the Wall at 8-30 a.m. where they will be met by 1 guide from each of the 12 positions accompanied by the 2 men of the 9th Cav. M.Gun Sqdrn. attached to these positions.

5. 2Lt Whitworth will remain in the CENTRE GROUP until the morning of the 31st Jany to ensure that everything is clearly understood by incoming officers.

   1 reliable man from each of the 73rd M.Gun Coy teams will be left in their respective positions until the morning of the 31st to ensure that the incoming teams clearly understand their duties etc.

6. 2Lt Shillito will relieve 2Lt Forsdike and will be in charge of R.32 & R.33.

7. For the purposes of handing over the 12 guns will be divided into the following 3 groups:-
   RIGHT GROUP. will include S.11. S.12. S.13.a. R.24.
   CENTRE GROUP. will include S.14. S.15. R.27. R.28. R.29.
   LEFT GROUP. will include R.30. R.31. F.1.

8. Officers will hand over a complete list of trench stores in their respective sectors, and obtain a receipt from the relieving officer for them.

   N.C.Os will also hand over all trench stores in their positions to the relieving N.C.O giving him a list and obtaining a receipt for them.

9. All work in hand and proposed will be handed over with the exception of work in progress at R.27.a. & S.13.a. which will be carried on by 73rd M.Gun Coy.

10. Officers are responsible that all dugouts and emplacements are left clean particular attention being paid to sanitation.

11. When handing over the officer in charge of the right sector must not forget the following unoccupied emplacements:- R.22. R.23. R.25. R.26. S.13.

12. On relief teams will convey gun equipment and company property to R.23. where it will be dumped under the supervision of Cpl Mahon. Cpl Mahon will remain with his team at R.23 to act as guard until the limbers arrive in the evening.

13. 2Lt Whitworth and the 1 man left at each position will leave the line at 7 a.m. on the 31st Jany and proceed to company headquarters.

Issued at 7-30 p.m.   (Signed) C.E.R.Croager, Lieutenant,
28th Jany. 1917.   Commanding 73 Company Machine Gun Corps.

Copy No. 1. 73rd I.B.   Copy No. 6. File.   Copy No. 11. 2Lt Andrews.
        2. O.C.9th Sqdn.   7. Lt Croager.   12. Lt Forsdike.
        3. War Diary.   8. Lt Bell.   13. 2Lt Shillito.
        4. War Diary.   9. Lt Tibbitt.   14. O.S.M.
        5. War Diary.   10. 2Lt Whitworth.   15. O.Mess.

73rd Machine Gun Company.   Copy No. _____

Amendment to OPERATION ORDER No. 26.
Para 5.
  (First Sub-para.) Delete from " until" to "Jany".

  (Second Sub-para.) Delete from" until " to "31st".

      ===================

Para. 13.
    Deleted.

      ===================

        (sgd) C.E.R.Croager. Lt.
     Commanding 73rd Machine Gun Company.

  73rd Machine Gun Company.   Copy No. _____
Para 5.Amendment to OPERATION ORDER No 26.

Army Form C. 2118.

WAR DIARY
or
INTELLIGENCE SUMMARY.
(Erase heading not required.)

Vol XI

War Diary of
47th Machine Gun Company
for the month of
February 1917.

WAR DIARY
or
INTELLIGENCE SUMMARY

Army Form C. 2118.

Place	Date	Hour	Summary of Events and Information	Remarks and references to Appendices
LES BREBIS	1/2/17		Company training carried out during morning & afternoon.	C.R.E.
"	2		1 O.R. granted leave to U.K. to 12th inst.	
"	3		Sections drilled with the gun &c.	C.R.E.
"	4		Working party of 1 officer and 30 O.R. to be found every night until further orders for the Royal Engineers (in the line)	
"	5		1 O.R. evacuated to C.C.S. The two remaining teams on the line relieved by two teams from billets (as per operation order No. 27 attached)	C.R.E.
"			1 O.R. granted leave to U.K. to 15th inst. 2 O.R. discharged from hospital.	
"	6		1 O.R. (No. 30965 L/Cpl. Bandey J.R.) proceeded to U.K. to take a commission. 1 O.R. admitted to hospital and evacuated to C.C.S. 1 O.R. admitted to hospital. 1 O.R. rejoined the company from 1 months probation at the Ordnance Mobile Workshop Bethune.	C.R.E.
"	7		1 O.R. admitted to hospital.	C.R.E.

Army Form C. 2118.

WAR DIARY
or
INTELLIGENCE SUMMARY.
(Erase heading not required.)

Instructions regarding War Diaries and Intelligence Summaries are contained in F. S. Regs., Part II. and the Staff Manual respectively. Title pages will be prepared in manuscript.

Place	Date	Hour	Summary of Events and Information	Remarks and references to Appendices
EGBRELS.	7.		1 O.R. granted leave to UK to 17th inst.	
"			1 O.R. returned to duty from a course at the Machine Gun School at Camiers.	C&P.g
"	8.		1 O.R. killed in action.	
"			1 O.R. evacuated to C.C.S.	
"	9.		1 O.R. proceed to join Headquarters Tanks on transfer to Heavy Section Machine Gun Corps.	
"			1 O.R. admitted to Hospital.	
"			1 O.R. wounded in action.	
"			Gun equipment re with two men per team of the 112th M.G. Coy. sent up to our two gun positions. Relief, by 112th M.G. Coy. of our two guns. (As per O.O. 26 attached). One of our per team & 1 officer remained in the line with new teams.	C&P.g
"	10		2 O.R. admitted to Hospital.	
"	10		1 O.R. evacuated to C.C.S.	C&P.g

WAR DIARY or INTELLIGENCE SUMMARY.

Army Form C. 2118.

(Erase heading not required.)

Instructions regarding War Diaries and Intelligence Summaries are contained in F. S. Regs., Part II. and the Staff Manual respectively. Title pages will be prepared in manuscript.

Place	Date	Hour	Summary of Events and Information	Remarks and references to Appendices
LES BREBIS	10.		2 O.R. joined from Base as reinforcements. Company received orders from Brigade H.Q. to proceed to NOEUX-les-MINES. Coy. started at 2.30 pm and arrived at 3.45 pm.	C.B.G.
NOEUX les MINES.	11		1 O.R. admitted to Hospital. 2 O.R. since sent to C.C.S.	
LABEUVRIERE	12.		Company ordered to move from billets in NOEUX les MINES to LABEUVRIERE starting at 9.0 AM and arriving at 12.0 noon. 1 O.R. Proceeded on leave to U.K. to take Commission. (No 6617 Sjt Railton H.) 2.Lt C.W. Scott & 2 O.R. proceed to Machine Gun School CAMIERS for a course of instruction.	C.B.G.
"	13			
"	14		Routes reconnoitred of country in search of training grounds. Major H. GILBERT rejoins Company from leave.	C.B.G.
"	15		Made arrangement re rifle & machine gun range. Company trained as usual & prepared for Inspection.	C.B.G.
"	16.		Inspection by Gen. NIVILLE, the Commander in Chief of French army. 2 O.R. admitted to Hospital.	C.B.G.

Army Form C. 2118.

WAR DIARY
or
INTELLIGENCE SUMMARY.
(Erase heading not required.)

Instructions regarding War Diaries and Intelligence Summaries are contained in F. S. Regs., Part II. and the Staff Manual respectively. Title pages will be prepared in manuscript.

Place	Date	Hour	Summary of Events and Information	Remarks and references to Appendices
MARŒUVRIERE	16.		Authority from H.Q.F.G.P. No 16520.B. dated 16/2/17 obtains for the issue of 1/- per diem working pay for the Company shoemaker.	C.E.R.E.
"	17.		2 OR discharged from hospital. Company training.	C.E.R.E.
"	18.		1 OR admitted to hospital.	C.E.R.E.
"	19.		1 OR joined the Company from the Base as a reinforcement. 1 OR admitted to hospital. Company training.	C.E.R.E.
"	21.		1 OR discharged from hospital. 1 OR admitted to hospital. Company did revolver & machine gun firing at the Range.	C.E.R.E.
"	22.		Firing on the range. A small scheme carried out. 6 OR joined the Company from the Base as reinforcements.	C.E.R.E.
"	23.		Staff ride for all Officers. Scheme carried out during morning followed by a lecture in the afternoon.	C.E.R.E.
"	24.		1 OR discharged from hospital.	C.E.R.E.

WAR DIARY
or
INTELLIGENCE SUMMARY.

(Erase heading not required.)

Army Form C. 2118.

Place	Date	Hour	Summary of Events and Information	Remarks and references to Appendices
LAREUVRIERE	24		Route march with Transport followed by an attack re.	C.O.C.Q.
"	25		2/Lt SCOTT + 2 O.R. returned to duty from a course of instruction at Machine Gun School. CAMIERS.	
			5 O.R. returned to duty from a course of instruction at the Antiaircraft group 1st Army.	
"	26		1 O.R. discharged from hospital	C.O.C.Q.
			1 O.R. admitted from hospital.	
			1 O.R. proceeded on a course of instruction at the Machine Gun School, CAMIERS.	
"	27		Company drill re.	C.O.C.Q.
			3 O.R. admitted to hospital.	
			2 O.R. joined as reinforcements from the base.	
"	28		Company training re.	C.O.C.Q.
			30 O.R. inoculated.	
			2 copies of Programme of work attached.	

(signature)
MAJOR
COMMANDING No. 73 M.G. COY.
MACHINE GUN CORPS,

SECRET.   73rd MACHINE GUN COMPANY.   Copy No. 4
Ref.Sheet.
36 B 1/4,000   OPERATION ORDER No.27.

(1.) The following reliefs will take place in the line during afternoon of February 5th.

Sgt. Hubbard)	will relieve	L/C Findlay)	will relieve
L/C. March.)	R. 32 who	Pte Manton.)	R. 33. who
Pte. Reid.)	return to	Pte. Adams.)	return to
" Hain.)	billets.	Pte. Maycock.)	billets.

(2.) 2/Lt. Scott will relieve 2/Lt. Shillito.

(3.) Teams will leave Coy. Headquarters at 2.p.m. and will be accompanied by a limber as far as the "Iron Gates" MAROC, carrying gun equipment.

(4.) The following gun equipment will be taken into the line by each team:-

    1. Gun and gun case.
    1. Spare parts.
    1. Spare barrel.
    1. Condenser bag and tube.
    1. Oil case.
    1. Cleaning rod.
    1. "Very" Light pistol.

All other equipment will be handed over in the line.

(5.) Three men will accompany each team to assist in carrying gun equipment. These men will remain in the line until it is time to convey gun equipment to "Hatchetts" where it will be placed on the ration limber.

(6.) As soon as teams at R.32. & R.33. are relieved they will march out independently and report to C.S.M. on arrival at billets.

(7.) Lists of trench stores taken over by N.C.C's of incoming teams will be forwarded to Coy. Headquarters with the first daily report.

(8.) Officers in charge will hand over all work in progress and proposed.

        (sgd,) C. E. R. Croager. Lt.
    Commanding 73rd Machine Gun Company.

February 4th. 1917.
Issued at 3.p.m.

Copy No. 1. 73rd I. B.	Copy No. 7. Lt. Croager.
2. O.C.No I.M.G.Sq.	8. " Tibbitt.
(For information.)	9. " Bell.
3. War Diary.	10. 2/Lt. Scott.
4. " "	11. " Shillito.
5. " "	12. Q. S. M.
6. File.	13. Officers Mess.

SECRET.   73rd MACHINE GUN COMPANY.   Copy No.....
Ref. Sheet.
36.B.1/40,000.   OPERATION ORDER. No. 28.
                                                   Feb. 9th. 1917.

1.   The 2 guns of the 73rd M. G. Coy. at R. 32. and R.33.
will be relieved by 2 guns of the 112. M. G. Coy. on Feb. 10th.

2.   Guns and Equipment of the 112. M. G. Coy. will be taken
up to "Hatchetts" on the evening of the 9th inst, where they will
be carried to R. 32. and R. 33.

3.   Gun equipment of the 73rd M. G. Coy. will be conveyed to
"HATCHETTS", when equipment of the 112th M. G. Coy. is in position
The following, however, will be brought out by each team when
relieved on the 10th inst.
         1 Gun and case.
         1 Spare parts.

4.   1 man from 112th M. G. Coy. will be attached to each of
the two positions on the night of the 9th/10th.

5.   The relieving teams will arrive at the "Hole in the wall"
at 8.a.m. where they will be met by one guide from each position.

6.   2/Lt. Scott and one man per team will remain in the line
until the morning of the 11th inst, to ensure that everything is
clearly understood by the relieving teams.

7.   2/Lt. Scott will hand over a complete list of trench
stores to the relieving Officer for the two guns, and obtain a receipt
for the same.
         N. C. O's i/c of teams will hand over all trench stores
in their respective positions and obtain a receipt for them from
the relieving N. C. O.

8.   All work in progress and proposed, including the dug-outs
at R. 37a and S.13a, will be handed over by the Officer in charge

9.   On relief teams, with the exception of the men detailed
in para. 6., will march out independently and report to C. S. M. on
arrival at Coy. Hd. Qtrs.

10.   Relief to be complete by 10.a.m.

11.   Working parties at S.13a. will leave the line at 5.p.m.
on the 9th inst. and will report to the C. S. M. on arrival at Coy.
Hd. Qtrs.

Issued at 2.30.p.m.
  9/2/17.   (sgd.) C. E. R. Croager, Lt.
                     Commanding 73rd Machine Gun Company.

     Copy No. 1. 73rd. I. B.   Copy No.7. File
              2. O.C. 112. M.G.Coy.   8. Lt. Croager.
              3. O.C. 9 Cav.M.G.Co.   9. Lt. Tibbitt.
              4. War Diary .   10. Lt. Bell.
              5.   "   "   11. 2/Lt. Scott.
              6.   "   "   12. C. S. M.
                          13. Officers Mess.

1/3 Coy. Machine Gun Corps. Programme of Work.

Week ending 24/2/17.

Day	8:30 – 9:30 am	9:30 – 10:30 am	10:45 – 11:45	11:45 – 12:45	2:0 – 3:0 pm	3:0 pm Night Work	Remarks
Monday	M. Gun Drill.	Infantry Drill in Sections / P.T.	Revolver Practice	Mechanism and Stoppages	Mechanism and Stoppages		I. During Infantry Drill and M. Gun Drill awkward squads will be formed whenever possible.
Tuesday	Company Drill. (Inft. Drill.)	Mechanism and Stoppages	Revolver Practice	Wagon Drill.	P.T.	Short lecture by Section officers to N.C.O.'s and men.	II. NCO's classed for backward N.C.O.'s will also be formed.
Wednesday	Firing on Range. (Stoppages)	Revolver Shooting on Range.	Advanced Gun Drill.	Company Drill. (Inf. Drill)		2 hours.	III. N.C.O's will be lectured by C.O. or qualified officers when not required during periods of elementary drill.
Thursday	Firing on Range. (Stoppages)	Revolver Shooting on Range.	J.D.	Small Scheme on ground near Range to include Operation Order. Taking up Position. Description of Targets			IV. Unless otherwise determined Friday's work will include lecture or attack practice on open fighting, and firing on Range.
Friday							V. The C.O will lecture the Subaltern Officers for ½ – 1 hr each evening. This lecture will include a discussion of the next day's work.
Saturday	8:30 – 9 Route march with troops to training ground.	9 – 10 Attack practice M. Guns advancing in Infantry Waves.	10 – 11:15 Taking up position after attack according to Operation Order.	11:15 – 12:15 Consolidation & Improvement of Position. Lecture on Same.	12:15 Lecture to Coy on Work Done. by C.O.	12:15 – 12:45 March back to Billets	

73rd. Machine Gun Company.

Programme of Training for Week Ending March 3rd 1917.

Day.	8.30 – 9.30	9.30 – 10.30	10.30 – 11.30	11.30 – 12.30	2.0 – 3.0	Night Work	REMARKS.
Monday	Company Drill. (Infantry Drill)	Attack Practice.	Consolidation of M.G. position	Revolver Practice.	Mechanism & Stoppages	2 hour.	With the exception of Thursday and Friday, all morning work will be at:— D.10.c.9.5. Ref. 36.B.N.E.
Tuesday.	Company Drill. (Infantry Drill)	Wagon Drill	M.G. drill on rough ground.	Bomb Throwing	Mechanism & Stoppages		
Wednesday	Company Drill (Infantry Drill)	Revolver Practice	Attack practice and consolidation of M.G. positions.				
Thursday.	Route March				P.T.	Lecture on the Attack	
Friday.							
Saturday.	Company Drill (Infantry Drill)	M.G. drill on rough ground.	Attack practice and Consolidation of M.G. positions.				

Army Form C. 2118.

WAR DIARY
or
INTELLIGENCE SUMMARY.
(Erase heading not required.)

Vol 12

Place	Date	Hour	Summary of Events and Information	Remarks and references to Appendices
France			War Diary for the month of March 1919 of 43rd Machine Gun Company	

Army Form C. 2118.

WAR DIARY
or
INTELLIGENCE SUMMARY.
(Erase heading not required.)

Instructions regarding War Diaries and Intelligence Summaries are contained in F. S. Regs, Part II. and the Staff Manual respectively. Title pages will be prepared in manuscript.

Place	Date	Hour	Summary of Events and Information	Remarks and references to Appendices
LABEUVRIÈRE	MARCH 1st		1 O.R. discharged from Hospital. 1 O.R. admitted to Hospital.	
"	" 2		2 2nd Lts PHILPOTT and 1 O.R. (Servant) returned to duty from a course at the A.A. Group 1st Army. The Company moved from LABEUVRIÈRE starting at 9.30 am and arrived at HAILLICOURT 12.0 noon. Full marching order. C.O. & Lt TIBBITT visits the 1st Canadian M.G.Coy at NOULETTE WOOD - went round the line. SOUCHEZ RIGHT & LEFT SECTOR. 1 O.R. discharged from Hospital.	C.E.L.C. C.E.R.C. C.O.R.C.
HAILLICOURT	" 3		Coy paraded for inspection of arm Returns, Equipment etc.	
"	" 4		Company moved from HAILLICOURT to FOSSE 10 where they had a meal. 10 Gun teams sent up to the trenches with three officers from FOSSE 10 at dusk while the remainder of the Company & T.H.Q. moved into Huts at NOULETTE WOOD. The Transport & Servants at FOSSE 10. (See O.O. No 29 as attaches).	C.E.R.C. C.E.L.C.
"	" 5		1 O.R. discharged from Hospital.	

2353 Wt. W2544/1454 700,000 5/15 D. D. & L. A.D.S.S./Forms/C. 2118.

Army Form C. 2118.

WAR DIARY
or
INTELLIGENCE SUMMARY.
(Erase heading not required.)

Instructions regarding War Diaries and Intelligence Summaries are contained in F. S. Regs., Part II. and the Staff Manual respectively. Title pages will be prepared in manuscript.

Place	Date	Hour	Summary of Events and Information	Remarks and references to Appendices
BOUZLETTE WOOD	6		1 O.R. admitted to Hospital.	
"	7		2000 Rounds fired on hostile dumps re.	C.R.C.
"	8		2 N.C.Os. withdrawn from the line & replaced for interviews by C.M.G.O. 3000 rounds fired at Enemy's back areas	
"	9		2 N.C.Os. sent to the U.K. as Instructors (Authy R.F. No. W.G.3728/9A of 21-2-17).	
			2 O.R. returned from a course of Signalling at R.E. School BEAUVEMONT.	C.R.C.
"	10		4 Reinforcements arrived from No 2 Sector A.S.C. HHTC (for Transport duties)	
			Away to a raid made on our front we fired 9000 rounds. The raid was unsuccessful.	C.R.C.
"	12		3 O.R. discharged from Hospital.	
"	13		An inter section relief took place in the line at night. In all four officers with the new teams (as per B.O. No 30 attached together with Appendix.)	C.R.C.
"	14		4 B O.R.S. attached to Company for Rations recommendation (Observers from 24th Divisional Scouts).	C.R.C.

Army Form C. 2118.

WAR DIARY
or
INTELLIGENCE SUMMARY.
(Erase heading not required.)

Instructions regarding War Diaries and Intelligence Summaries are contained in F. S. Regs., Part II. and the Staff Manual respectively. Title pages will be prepared in manuscript.

Place	Date	Hour	Summary of Events and Information	Remarks and references to Appendices
Noulette Wood	15.		1 Sgt. sent to U.K. to take up a Commission (authy W.O. Telegram 840 A.G. 100/M.C./61. of 27/12/16. 4850 rounds in Artillery fire	
"	16		10 new dugouts and gun positions started in connection with defence Scheme 3.	C.E.S.G.
"	#16		6250 rounds fired indirect.	
"	17		4 O.R.s attached to the Company for rations accommodation (observers from 24th Divisional Scouts).	
			1 O.R. admitted to hospital.	
			1 O.R. killed in action. 1 rank killed by shell. 1 O.R. above mentioned buried in Aix-Noulette.	
"	18		2 O.R. sent to sent to M.G. Corps Base Depot on unfit for service at the Front. (Authy. H.Q. 44071, of. 19/1/17	C.E.S.G.
"	19		2 N.C.O.s sent to the return from school courier for a course.	C.E.S.G.
			1 O.R. returned from " " " from " "	C.E.S.G.
			2 O.R.s attached to 197th Coy M.G.C. on orders.	C.E.S.G.

Army Form C. 2118.

WAR DIARY
or
INTELLIGENCE SUMMARY.
(Erase heading not required.)

Instructions regarding War Diaries and Intelligence Summaries are contained in F. S. Regs., Part II. and the Staff Manual respectively. Title pages will be prepared in manuscript.

Place	Date	Hour	Summary of Events and Information	Remarks and references to Appendices
OULETTE WOOD	19/3		2 ORs returned from 197" Coy A.S.C.	
"	20		1 OR admitted to hospital	C.E.G.
"	21		1 OR evacuated to C.C.S.	
"			1 OR discharged from hospital	C.E.G.
"			4 ORs arrived from Machine Gun Corps Base Depot as reinforcements	
"	22		2 ORs admitted to hospital	C.E.G.
"			6000 rounds fired at enemy's back areas.	
"			Leave relieve in the line (as per operation order No 31 attached)	
"	23		Indirect firing carried out (6250 rounds)	C.E.G.
"			1 OR discharged from hospital	
"	24		4 reinforcements arrived from No 2 A.S.C. Section A.H.T.D. (Transport drivers)	C.E.G.
"			Application made to Tryah & Gaunts by them for the issue of 12 known stores to the Company. This has been of great use to the Company in keeping emplacements water sealed.	
"	25		13,250 rounds fired in conection with a raid made by the am	C.E.G.

WAR DIARY or INTELLIGENCE SUMMARY

Army Form C. 2118.

Place	Date	Hour	Summary of Events and Information	Remarks and references to Appendices
HOULETTE WOOD	25/3		Infantry Battn in the Brigade on our right.	OCRG
"	26/3		1 O.R. proceeded to report to Rly Signal Officer at ABBEVILLE (withy 2nd Division) AW 9692 24/3/17.	OCRG
"	27		1 O.R. admitted to hospital. In cooperation with a raid on our left we fired 18,250 rounds.	OCRG
"	28		1 O.R. evacuated to 33rd C.C.S. 2 O.R. sent to UK to take up commission	OCRG
"	30		Three guns relieved by the 17th A.G. Coy. Three gun position evacuated. Wire position taken over from the 10th Canadian M.G. Coy	OCRG
"	30			

CCRCogh? Major
OC 73rd M.G. Coy 31/3/17

Secret.
Ref.Map
36.b.3 Ed.
1:40,000.

73 Company Machine Gun Corps.

Copy No...... 6

OPERATION ORDER No.29.

March 4th, 1917.

1. The 73rd Machine Gun Company will relieve the 1st Can.M.Gun Coy on March 4th as per table below:-

Pos.	Strength	N.C.O.	Officer	Guides at	Section	
3.	4 men.	1.	1 officer at pos.6.	Company dump	4.	2Lt Forsdike.
4.	4 men.	1.				
9.	4 men.	2.	1 officer at pos.9.	French dump.	2	2Lt Philpott.
10.	4 men.					
11.	4 men.	1.				
12.	4 men.					
5.	4 men.	1.	1 officer at pos.6.	Company dump	1.	2Lt Whitworth.
6.	4 men.	1.				
7.	4 men.					
8.	4 men.	1.				

2. All teams going into the line and personnel going into NOULETTE WOOD will leave FOSSE 10 at a time to be notified.(Approx.5 p.m.) There will be 1 guide for teams 2,4,5,6,7 & 8 to Company dump.
" " " 1 " " " 9,10,11 & 12 to French dump.
Remainder of company will leave for NOULETTE WOOD Huts under Lt Tibbitt.

3. Officers above mentioned will reconnoitre their new positions in the early afternoon under arrangements to be notified. Their servants should accompany Teams 6 & 9.

4. Teams will take into the line 12 belts, Mark IV tripod and minimum gun equipment, and rations for 5th March. Arrangements re carriers will be notified later.

5. Section officers will hand to C.S.M. team lists and names of carriers with each team, by 3 p.m.

6. Lists of trench stores (checked) will be sent to H.Q. by returning ration limbers on the night 5/6th March.

7. Officers must be careful to take over trench maps, as new copies are not yet available. The following information must be carefully taken over:- Positions of ration dumps, Water arrangements, Indirect fire targets, Work in hand and proposed.
Ration dumps will be as used by 1st Can. Coy till otherwise notified. Indirect fire will be carried on as per 1st Can.Coy. programme.

8. All carriers will be instructed to return to the Church, AIX NOULETTE, whence they will be guided to NOULETTE WOOD HUTS.

9. Officers i/c Sections will report relief complete by returning carriers.

10. Coy. Headquarters will be at NOULETTE WOOD HUTS, Approx. R.28.c.

11. Until further information is gained route Trenches-Coy Hd Qrs is:- ARRAS ROAD TRENCH - AIX NOULETTE- Tramway line to huts.

Issued at 1 p.m.
(Sd) H.Gilbert, Major,
Commanding 73 Coy, Machine Gun Corps.

Copy No. 1-2....1st Can. M.Gun. Coy.
3......73rd Infantry Brigade.
4-6....War Diary.
7......File.
8......C.O.
9-17...Each officer.
18.....C.S.M.

Secret.
Ref. Sheet.
56.c. S.W.3.

Copy No....3.....

73rd MACHINE GUN COMPANY.

OPERATION ORDER. NO. 30.

(1) The following reliefs will take place during night of 13th inst.
    (a) No. 3. Section will relieve No. 1 Section at Positions No. 5, 6, 7, and 8.
    (b) No 4 Section will relieve itself at Nos 2 and 4 positions.
    (c) The teams at Nos. 11 and 12 positions will remain there.
    (d) The teams at present in Nos. 5 and 6 positions will relieve those at No. 9. and 10.
Thus teams at present in Nos. 7, 8, 9, 10, 2 and 4 will return to billets.

(2) 2/Lt Scott and 2/Lt Shillito will live in HUDSON TRENCH.
Lt. Tibbitt and 2/Lt Andrews do. do. NORTH ALLEY.
Officers supervision of teams is as detailed in Appendix. A.
2/Lt. Scott's work will be notified. Officers will leave billets for the line in the afternoon at a time to be notified.

(3) Teams of Nos. 3 and 4 sections will march off from billets at approximately 6.30.p.m. Guides from positions 5, 6, 7, & 8 will wait at COMPANY DUMP at 7.30.p.m. The 2 guns of No. 4. Section going into the line will provide their own guides.

(4) As soon as Nos. 5 & 6 positions have been relieved the relieved teams will proceed to Positions 9 & 10 under arrangements to be made by 2/Lt. Whitworth.

(5) Only the following gun equipment will be taken from one position to another, or from positions to billets.
Gun, Gun-case, Spare Parts, Oil Case, Cleaning Rod, and one Very light pistol. All the other equipment will be handed over and shewn on Trench Store report.

(6) Teams proceeding to the line will take up with them the above mentioned gun equipment.

(7) Teams from Nos. 7, 8, 9, 10, 2 & 4 positions, on relief will find limbers waiting at PULP HOUSE. Teams from positions 9 & 10, being the last to be relieved, will use the half limber.

(8) Returning teams will march with limbers (as guide to billets) and on arrival will report to the C.S.M.

(9) Separate orders have been issued to the Transport Officer.

(10) Lists of Trench stores taken over by incoming N.C.O's will be forwarded to Coy H.Q. with the first daily report.

(11) Every care must be taken by N.C.O's and men i/c of teams to hand over all information concerning the gun position, water supply, ration dump, and in particular, portions of the trenches which are under observation of the enemy.

(12) Relieving Officers will pay special attention to Appendix A, before making up their teams. Team lists will be handed to the C.S.M. by 6.c.p.m. on the 12th inst.

(13) During the coming tour of duty in the line indirect fire will only be carried out on orders from Coy. H.Q. unless work in Appendix A is impossible.

(14) Reference Appendix A., all teams in the line, should if possible include a practical workman.

(15) Appendix A. gives a complete idea of the work it is intended to carry out on this front with regard to Vickers Guns

(16) Before going into the line each Officer will study the map of proposed positions, take down map locations, and notes on fields of fire.

(17) Apprndix B. should be carefully studied.

Issued at 5.p.m.
12/3/17.

(Sgd,) H. Gilbert, Major,
Commanding 73rd Machine Gun Company.

Copy No. 1. 73rd I. B.
     2. War Diary
     3. do.
     4. do.
     5. File.
     6. C. C.

Copy No. 7. Lt. Croager.
     8. Lt. Tibbitt.
     9. Lt. Bell.
     10. 2/Lt. Scott.
     11. 2/Lt. Shillito.
     12. 2/Lt. Andrews.

Copy No.13 2/Lt Forsdi[?]
     14. 2/Lt. Philpott.
     15. 2/Lt. Whitworth.
     16. C. S. M.
     17. Sgt. Evans.
     18. Cpl Dunkley.

APPENDIX A. (Continued.)

Team.	Pos. to be made.	Personnel.	Officer i/c	Work to be done. (In order.)	Remarks.
9.	L.	1 NCO. 5 men.	2/Lt. Shillito.	Deep dugout in RATION Tr. or near. Good open emplm.	Teams lives at present position till deep dugout is finished. This can be worked in day time. 3 sentries left on.
10.	K.	1 NCO. 5 men.	do.	Finish deep dugout. Good open emplmt. Deepen Com. with RATION Tr.	Night work. 3 sentries left on gun.
11.	J.	1 NCO. 5 men.	do.	Deepen shallow trenches in vicinity to hide future movements of team. Temp. Shelter. Rough open emplmt. Deep dugout. Good open emplmt.	Night work. 3 sentries left on gun.
12.	Q.	1 NCO 4 men.	2/Lt. Andrews.	Shell hole. Communication trench to shell hole. Deepen lateral trench. Deep dugout.	Night work. No sentry need be left on gun.

APPENDIX. B.

(1) <u>Temporary Shelters</u>. Size about 6' by 8' Corrugated iron supported. 2 sandbags layer on top. Should take about 3 nights to build. Or use old dugout.

(2) Guns detailed for indirect fire will each fire about 3000 rds during the night at times to be appointed by the supervising officer.

(3) <u>Deep Dugouts</u>. Start with the alternative entrance, i.e. not the one which is to be opposite the battle emplacement. Frames will be 6' long 3' wide giving an internal width of 2' 6 inches. Gradient of entrance will be in all cases 2 in 3.

(4) Supervising Officers should endeavour to do 4 - 6 hrs work every night with each team, depending in distance of team from work.

(5) Every attention must be paid to concealment. Teams should be instructed to use their ingenuity in imitating the surrounding scheme of cover as closely as possible.

(6) Every effort must be made to further the scheme of work. Supervising Officers will send in to Coy. H. Q. a daily report.

APPENDIX A. issued with 73rd MACHINE GUN COMPANY OPERATION ORDER No.30.

Team No.	Pos to be made.	Personnel.	Officer Supervising	Work to be done, (In order.)	Remarks.
3.	D.	1 NCO 4 men	2/Lt Andrews.	Rough open emplacement, Deepening adjacent trenches. Deep dug-out. Good open emplacement.	Night work. Team lives at present position until deep dugout is made. No sentry need be left on gun.
4.	J.	1 NCO 4 men	2/Lt Andrews.	Deepen adjacent trenches. Splinter proof shelter Deep Dugout. Good open emplacement.	Team lives at present position till shelter is made. Night work only till deep dugout is started. 1 sentry left on gun till team lives in shelter.
5.	K.	1 NCO 4 men	Lt. Tibbitt.	Cut trench into BAJOLLE Temp. shelter in BAJOLLE. Rough open emplacement Deep dugout in BAJOLLE. Deep dugout Good open Emplacement.	Team lives at present position till shelter is made. Night work only till deep dugout is started. 1 sentry left on gun till team lives in shelter.
6.	E.	1 NCO 4 men	Lt. Tibbitt.	Tem. shelter Rough open emplmt. Deep dugout. Communication to BAJOLLE.	Night work till deep dugout is started. 1 sentry left with gun in present position till shelter is occupied.
7.	F.	1 NCO 5 men	Lt. Tibbitt.	Rough open emplmt in RIVER ALLEY Tem. shelter or cellar in vicinity. Deepen & repair RIVER ALLEY. Find good cellar or make deep dugout. Good open emplmt.	Night work. 2 sentries left with gun in present position till team shifts to the shelter.
8.	M.	1 NCO. 4 men.	do.	Good open emplmt at pres. alt. position. Better communication Better communication from there to Hd Qtrs. Trench.	Night work. 1 sentry left on gun Team remains in present dugout.
9.	L.	1 NCO 5 men	2/Lt Shillito.	Deep dugout in RATION Trench. Good open Emplmt.	Team lives at present position till deep is finished. This can be worked at in day time. 2 sentries left on gun

Secret.   Copy No... 3 ...
                     73rd MACHINE GUN COMPANY.

                     OPERATION ORDER No. 31.

(1.)   The following reliefs will take place during the night of 23rd inst.
         (a) No. 1. Section (3gun teams) will relieve No. 2. Section at
Nos. 11. & 12. positions.
         (b) No. 2. Section (2 gun teams) will relieve No. 1. Section at
9. and K. positions.
         (c) No. 4. Section will relieve the team at No. 10. position.
         (d) All other teams in the line will remain in their present
positions, i.e. D. J. E. 6. 7. 8.   Nos. K. 9. 10. 11. 12. teams will return
to billets.

(2.)   (a) 2/Lt. Scott will remain in the line until further notice.
         (b) 2/Lt. Philpott will relieve 2/Lt. Shillito in HUDSON TRENCH.
         (c) Lt. Tibbitt will remain in the line until further notice.
         (d) 2/Lt. Forsdike will relieve 2/Lt. Andrews in NORTH ALLEY.

(3.)   Teams of Nos. 1, 2, & 4. Sections will march off from billets at
6. 30. p.m.

(4.)   Officers will arrange that, in all ingoing teams, there is at least
1. man who can act as guide.

(5.)   Only the following Gun Equipment will be taken from 1 position to
another, or from positions to billets, or vice versa.:- Gun, Gun Case,
Condenser Bag and tube, Spare Barrel, Cleaning rod, and 1. "Very" light pistol.
         All other equipment will be handed over and shewn on the Trench
Store Report. Teams going into the line will take in with them the above
mentioned Gun Equipment. Greater care must be taken in regard to above para (5
(6.)   Outgoing teams will carry their guns etc. down to the PUMP HOUSE
where they will find the limbers waiting for them.

(7.)   Teams, after packing their gun equipment in the limbers will march
back to billets and report to C. S. M. on arrival.

(8.)   Separate orders have been issued to the Transport Officer.

(9.)   Lists of Trench Stores taken over by incoming N.C.O's will be
forwarded to Coy. H.Q. with the first daily report. It is of the utmost
importance that these lists are more carefully filled up and must be signed by
both the incoming and outgoing N.C.O.

(10.)   Every care must also be taken by N.C.O's i/c teams in the handing
over of his position ; all information concerning rations and water supply,
and in particular, any portion of trench which may be under observation of the
enemy.

(11.)   During the coming tour of duty indirect fire will only be carried
out from orders from H.Q.

(12.)   Special attention must be paid to the handing over of all work
proposed and in progress by Officers, and must be done in writing.

(13.)   All teams leaving billets must consist of the same number as those
being relieved in the line.

       Issued at 11.0. a.m.   Sgd. H. Gilbert, Major,
       23/5/17.   Commanding 73rd Machine Gun Company.

Copy. No. 1. 73. I. B.   No. 6. C. O.   No. 11. 2/Lt. Scott.
      No. 2. War Diary.   7. Lt. Croager.   12. 2/Lt. Shillito.
          3.   "   8. Lt. Bell.   13. 2/Lt. Forsdike.
          4.   "   9. Lt. Tibbitt.   14. 2/Lt. Philpott.
          5. File.   10. Lt. Andrews.   15. 2/Lt. Whitworth.
                         Copy No. 16. C. S. M.

73rd BRIGADE MACHINE GUN COMPANY

24th DIVISION

APRIL 1917

WAR DIARY
INTELLIGENCE SUMMARY

Army Form C. 2118.

Instructions regarding War Diaries and Intelligence Summaries are contained in F. S. Regs., Part II. and the Staff Manual respectively. Title pages will be prepared in manuscript.

(Erase heading not required.)

Place	Date	Hour	Summary of Events and Information	Remarks and references to Appendices
OULETTE HUTS	1st April		1 OR admitted and evacuated to CCS.	CORG
"	2		No of rounds fired on night of 1/2 7,000	
"	3		1 OR admitted to hospital	CORG
"	4		2/Lt PHILPOTT F.A. leave to UK.	
"	"		1 OR admitted to hospital	
"	"		1 OR admitted to hospital. Indirect firing done on back areas 6000 rds.	
"	"		2 ORs admitted to hospital	
"	5		1 OR admitted & evacuated to CCS.	CORG
"	6		5 ORs reported from the Base as reinforcements.	
"	"		1 OR discharged from hospital	
"	"		2 ORs evacuated to CCS.	
"	7		1 OR admitted to hospital	CORG
"	"		1 OR evacuated to CCS.	
"	8		2 ORs returned to duty from a course of instruction at CAMIERS.	CORG
"	"		1 OR evacuated to CCS.	
"	9		1 OR discharged from hospital	CORG

WAR DIARY
or
INTELLIGENCE SUMMARY.

(Erase heading not required.)

Army Form C. 2118.

Place	Date	Hour	Summary of Events and Information	Remarks and references to Appendices
MEULETTE HUTS	10		4th Casualty leaves France with Infantry for an attack on BOIS EN HACHE	
"	11		" went into the line. Final preparations made in the line for the attack on BOIS EN HACHE.	
			2 ORs killed in action	CBCG
			2 ORs wounded in action	CBCG
			1 OR arrives from the Base as a reinforcement.	
"	12	6.0am	2 Lt FOSDIKE J.F. wounded, preliminary attack on BOIS EN HACHE took place	
			Distribution of guns re a for material attached.	
			2 Lt FOSDIKE J.E. wounded in action	
			3 ORs killed in action	
			3 ORs wounded in action	
			2 ORs reported missing	
			1 OR previously reported missing now reported killed	
			1 OR " " " wounded	
			1 OR " " " missing	
			1 OR " " " wounded	
			1 OR wounded in action	CBCG

Army Form C. 2118.

WAR DIARY
or
INTELLIGENCE SUMMARY.
(Erase heading not required.)

Instructions regarding War Diaries and Intelligence Summaries are contained in F. S. Regs., Part II. and the Staff Manual respectively. Title pages will be prepared in manuscript.

Place	Date	Hour	Summary of Events and Information	Remarks and references to Appendices
MOULETTE HUTS	13		Continuation of the advance.	O.B.G.
"	14		1 OR wounded in action	
"	15		1 OR died of wounds	
			1 OR admitted to Hospital	O.B.G.
			2 ORs evacuated to CCS.	
"	16		1 OR evacuated to CCS	
"	18		6 OR reports to Company from the Base as reinforcements	
"	19		2/Lt. STARROTT rejoined the Company from leave to U.K.	
"	20		Company relieves in the line by 139th Machine Gun Coy. Relief complete by 10.0 p.m. Coy billets in PETIT SAINS.	
PETIT SAINS.	21		2/Lt. GOURLAY G joined the Company as reinforcement from the Base.	O.B.G.
"	22		Company refitting	
MARLES LES MINES	23		Company moved to MARLES LES MINES no 8 Shoppers no Shoppers	O.B.G.
			" " LINGHEM.	
			21 ORs reported as reinforcement from the Base.	
LINGHEM.	24		1 OR proceeded to report to OC Transportation Troops Depot BOULOGNE Infantry Base, GHQ, CR No 67/45/2.17/106 A d/- 16/4/17.	O.B.G.

WAR DIARY or INTELLIGENCE SUMMARY

Army Form C. 2118.

Place	Date	Hour	Summary of Events and Information	Remarks and references to Appendices
LINGHEM	25		Company reorganising.	O.B.G.
"	26		" moved to AUCHEL. No Stragglers.	
			1 O.R. admitted to Hospital.	
AUCHEL	27		Company moved to NOEUX les MINES. no Stragglers.	
NOEUX les MINES	28		2 O.R. admitted to Hospital	
			Company commenced training	
			1 O.R. admitted to Hospital	
"	29		1 O.R. discharged from Hospital	O.B.G.
			2nd Lt. P. HERBOTT F.A. 1 Servant + 1 O.R. to course of instruction to CAMIERS.	
			Armourer rejoined to make up deficiencies in Section.	
"	30		2nd Lt. C. W. SCOTT. admitted to Hospital	O.B.G.
			2 N.C.O.s arrived from the Base for exchange.	

Burkett
Major
Commanding 73 Machine Gun Coy

H.G. 35.
April 29th 1917.

Brigade Major,
       73rd Infantry Brigade.

Reference your B.M. 495 dated 22/4/17, herewith the required narrative please.

April. 11th.

Distribution of Vickers Guns.

1. ....7 Guns in defensive positions, covering SOUCHEZ VALLEY and Southern slopes of LORETTE SPUR. These guns formed the right half Company and were under the command of Lt. TIBBITT

2. ....4 teams (under Lt. WHITWORTH & 2/LT. ~~~~~~~ FORSDIKE) which had been selected and trained to atke part in the attack on the BOIS EN HACHE were in position in BAJOLLE TR. on the LORETTE SPUR as an extra precaution against hostile counter attack from the direction of BOIS D' HIRONDELLE. At approx. midnight 11/12th April these four guns moved to their assembly positions for the attack.

3. ....5 guns of 73rd M.G.Coy and 6 guns of 191 M.G.Coy (Attached to 73rd M.G.Coy.) were in defence positions on LORETTE SPUR. Indirect and overhead fire emplacements had beenmade, under supervision of 2/LT SCOTT, for all these guns, to deal with hostile counter attacks and also for covering fire for the attack on BOIS EN HACHE. 29.000 round S.A.A. per gun had been brought up for this purpose.

4. .... 2 guns of the 191. M.G.Coy remained in reserve in NOULETTE WOOD.

My battle headquarters was in BAJOLLE TR. on LORETTE SPUR.

Lt Croager was at Adv. Bde. H.Q. to act as Liaison Officer.

April 12th.

At Zero hour 5 a.m. for the attack on BOIS EN HACHE

1. ....2 guns under Lt. WHITWORTH co-operated with the left Batt 9th Batt Royal Sussex Rgt. Of these one gun remained in support in our old front line.

    1 gun moved to German front line with C.Coy. and took up a position on the right.

2. ....2 guns under 2/Lt FORSDIKE co-operated with the right Batt 2nd Leinster Rgt. Of these 1 gun reached its objective, viz; German front line.

    1 team with 2/Lt FORSDIKE suffered heavy casualties;

    2/Lt. FORSDIKE...........Wounded.

    4 men   killed.

    2 men   Wounded.

The gun and equipment were for the time being, lost.
From zero to zero plus 30 minutes heavy barrage firing was carried out be the eleven guns on the LORETTE SPUR, on accurately planned lines, which formed a complete box barrage round the objectives. From zero plus 30 minutes onwards through the day intermittent

fire was kept up to aid the infantry in consolidating.
Total number of rounds fired approx. 100000

April 13th.

Firing was continued intermittently on barrage lines and it was evident that our troops were consolidating.

Commencing at 9.a.m. I visited the three Battn. H.Q. and the three guns in the captured trenches. It was evident that an enemy retirement had taken place. I ordered all guns to cease fire. Total number of rounds fired had been brought up to 150,000.

Night 13/14th the seven guns in SOUCHEZ VALLEY were ordered to withdraw to NOULETTE WOOD and reorganise.

The eight guns of the 191 Company were withdrawn and returned to their Company.

April 14th.

The right half Company (7 guns under Lt. TIBBITT) arrived at NOULETTE WOOD from SOUCHEZ VALLEY about 7 a.m. in a rather exhausted condition. Lt. CROAGER (2nd i/c) made up two fresh teams from reserve men and details and proceeded to ANGRES and was attached firstly to 12th R.F. and later to 7th Northants. and took up positions in LIEVIN.

Lt WHITWORTH and his two guns were withdrawn from their old positions in the old German line and 2nd line to NOULETTE HUTS to reorganise. The surviving gun which had been attached to the 2nd Leinster Rgt was likewise withdrawn and placed under Lt. WHITWORTH.

My Company was by this time scattered and disorganised. I no longer attempted to keep Officers or teams in their right Section At 2.30.p.m. 2/Lt. SHILLITO and two guns received orders to report to the O.C. 7th Northants Rgt as soon as possible. These teams arrived at CITE DE L'ABBATOIR at dusk and were ordered to remain in close support at Southern extremity of the CITE DE L'ABBATOIR with a view to defending the Brigade Right Flank.

At 5.30.p.m. Lt. TIBBITT and three guns proceeded from NOULETTE WOOD to reserve positions in HEADQUARTERS TRENCH.

In the evening the 5 guns under 2/LT. ANDREWS on LORRETTE SPUR were withdrawn to NOULETTE HUTS and reorganised.

April. 15th.

Lt. CROAGER and 2/Lt. SHILLITO were in touch at 10.a.m. Lt. CROAGER and his two guns advanced to the CHATEAU just N. of BOIS DE RIAMONT and later advanced with the leading platoon of the 13th Middlesex Rgt to FOSSE 3. Several enemy snipers in houses were dealt with by these guns. At dusk the guns withdrew with the Infantry and took up defensive positions in the immediate vicinity of the CHATEAU. LT. CROAGER was in communication with the guns of the 17th I.B. in the CITE DE BOIS DE LIEVIN.

2/LT SHILLITO and two guns reported to the O.C. Mdx Rgt and moved into forward positions in houses in the CITE DE GARENNES.

In the afternoon of the 15th therefore there were 4 guns in the outpost line.

I ordered 1. Lt. TIBBITT and three guns in Hd.Qtrs Tr. with pack transport to CITE DE L'ABBATOIR and remain in support.

2. Lt. WHITWORTH and three guns (the rested assaulting teams to move from NOULETTE WOOD to

positions in reserve in Hd. Qtrs Trench. These guns arrived about 6.0.p.m.

April 16th.

Lt. TIBBITT & 3 guns arrived at CITE DE L'ABBATOIR at 4-30 and reported to O.C. Middlesex Rgt.
Atv 10-30 a.m. 2/Lt. SHILLITO moved his guns forward to commanding positions in front of CITE DE GARRENNES and fired several thousand rounds with direct sighting and observation at enemy snipers in CITE DE RIAUMONT. The hostile sniping was considerably reduced.

At 12. noon I ordered Lt. WHITWORTH and three guns in HEADQUARTERS to move forward in closer reserve in CITE DE L'ABBATOIR.

I visited O.C. Middlesex at his forward H.Q. and arrang-ed that Lt. WHITWORTH and his three guns should relieve the four guns in the outpost line.

This relief was carried out and the sitaation on the night 16/17 was:-

- LT. WHITWORTH. (1 gun in CHATEAU N.of BOIS DE RIAU MONT
  (2 guns in the CITE DE GARENNES.

- 2/Lt. SHILLITO   3 guns in CITE DE L'ABBATOIR in close reserve.

- Lt. TIBBITT.   3 guns in CITE DE L'ABBATOIR in close support.

- LT CROAGER and one team (depleated by reason of casualties) to Hd. Qtrs Trench.

April 17th.

Lt. CROAGER returned to FOSSE IO to carry on administrative work.
Lt. TIBBITT organized defensive positions in the RIVER LINE for his three support guns.

At. 5-30.p.m. I ordered

1. Lt. TIBBITT with three guns to reinforce the three guns in the outpost line.

2/Ltm SHILLITO to move forward from reserve to @ support in the CITE DE L'ABBATOIR.

E. 2/Lt ANDREWS and six guns to move from NOULETTE WOOD to reserve positions in HD.Qtrs Trench.

These orders were carried out, and the sitaation on night of 17/18th April was :-

- Lt. WHITWORTH (1 gun with Infantry Post South of CITE DE
  (GARENNES.
  (2 guns in CITE DE GARRENNES.

- Lt. TIBBITT. (1 gun with Infantry post in BOIS DE RIAMONT
  (2 guns in CHATEAU N. of Bois DE RIAMONT.

April 18th.

No alteration in the situation.

2/Lt. SHILLITO in consultation with the O.C. Middlesex Rgt worked and put into operation a scheme of defence by Vickers guns of the RIVER LINE (CITE DE L'ABBATOIR.)

April 19th.   At 5-30.a.m. Lt. TIBBIT'S guns fired approximately
1,000 rounds in support of a minor operation carried out
by the 7th Northants Rgt.

April 20th   Relief by the 139th M.G.Coy was completed by 10.0.p.m.
All personnel of the 73rd Machine Gun Company marched
to billets in PETIT SAINS.

            Sgd. H. Gilbert, Major,
Commanding 73rd Machine Gun Company.

30th April. 1917.

OPERATION ORDER.
by
Major H. Gilbert. M.C.

Commanding 73rd Machine Gun Company.

Lt. Croager,
The following will probably give you some idea of
what has happened, what is going to happen, and what I want ΘΘ you to
do.
The 139th Company were sent back by mistake. I do not
know whether you met them at 1.p.m. to day - at any rate our arrangements
were all correct.
They are coming again to-morrow 19th inst and are due
at the Bde. H.Q. at the QUARRY in the Arras Road at 1.p.m. Can you
please arrange guides for them to advanced Bde. H.Q. The Bde. O.O. says
1. Officer and 1 guide per platoon. I think you had better guide them
yourself and take four other men. One of their sections may be remaining
behind or going on to MARQUEEEEE. At any rate they must move off by
Sections with 100 yds interval.
In case you do not know the best route, it is as follows
Colonel's House - Cross roads at M.26.c.8.2. - M.26.d.8.2. - M.33.a.
4½ 9. thence to Bde. H.Q.
From Bde. H.Q. I am arranging guires to destination.
As far as I know their 12 guns are coming up tonight
and I am putting them in a cellar in CITE de lABBATOIR. In case a
mistake occurs remember that their limbers can come up with their sections
at least as far as RED MILL by day.
Then about our coming out. I am enclosing a note to Lt.
Bell, which please read and send to him.
I have asked Scott to make arrangements for the
accommodation of the whole Company in NOULETTE HUTS on night 19/20th.
The Brigade orders are for us to await further move orders there.
Will you please make complete arrangements and withdraw
Andrews and guns now in Head Quarters Trench to NOULETTE HUTS after dusk
night 19/20th. You may withdraw any details you like during the day.
On returning, guns and all equipment may be kept in the
wagon lines at FOSSE IO until morning of the 20th.
After you have guided 139th Company to Advanced Bde H.Q.
I think you yourself had better return to FOSSE IO and commence to clear up
the mess we are in. Are you clear about everything, or do you want any
more information. If you do want more information, please send a man back
with pte. Sharp.
18/4/17.
9.30.p.m.   Sgd. H. Gilbert, Major.
Commanding 73rd Machine Gun Company.

OPERATION ORDER,
by Major. H. Gilbert, M.C.
Commanding 73rd Machine Gun Company.

Lt. Bell,
Our relief arrangements to-day seem to have got into a
muddle but at any rate we are being relieved by to-morrow night 19/20th.
On coming out of the line, guns and equipment will be
kept in wagons at FOSSE IO until morning of the 20th .
It is possible that we are start marching to back areas
sometime in the 20th.

The 139th Coy. (Sections - I do not know about transport.)
will arrive at Bde. H.Q. QUARRY at 1.p.m. to-morrow 19th. Can you get in
touch with T.O. and give him some information.

Re Transport for our men coming out. I think limbers
would be best as the roads are now improved. Wagon covers should be on all
limbers. Best route is as follows :-

page. 2.

Colonels house - Cross roads at M.26.a.8.2. - M.26.d.8.2 - M.33a.2.8. M.33.a.4.39. thence to Advm Bde. H.Q. thence to RED MILL. The whole route can be used by daylight.
We should want these full limbers as per below.
  1 full limbers for Shillito's these guns now are in Cité de L'ABBATOIR.

  2 full limbers for Whitworth's and Tibbitt's 3 guns each now in the front line.

  to be at RED MILL at 12. p.m.

The mens packs will be carried on the limbers. RED MILL is, I think a good place to wait and I have arranged times as above so that there ought to be no waiting. The two limbers for the six guns must be sure to collect evrything before leaving.

To-morrow night Company rations to be delivered to C.S.M. at NOULETTE HUTS.

Do you want any other information. If you don, send your note back to Croager by this orderly and Croager will arrange to pass on to me.

please let the Sergeant Major see this note.

  18/4/17. Sgd. H. Gilbert. Major.
 9.30.p.m. Commanding 73rd Machine Gun Company.

OPERATION ORDER.
by
Major. H. Gilbert, M.C.
Commanding 73rd Machine Gun Company.

Lt. Tibbitt. (i/c. Front line guns, 4, 5, & 6.)

Lt. Whitworth (i/c. do do do 1, 2, & 3.)
2/Lt. Shillito.
Lt. Bell.
Lt. Croager.
O.C. 139. M.G.Coy.
C.S.M. 73rd M.G.Coy.

  The 139th Coy were due to arrive in ANGRES to day 18th to relieve us, but someone sent them back in error. However they are trying again to-morrow and our relief should be complete by midnight 19/20
  The following instructions will hold good unless you hear to the contrary.
1. 12 guns and a guard of the 139th Company will arrive at Advm Bde. H.Q. night 18/19th and stored in a cellar in Cité de L'ABBATIOR under arrangements to be made by me.

2. 3 Sections of 139th M.G.Coy arrive Adv. Bde. H.Q. at approx 2.0.p.m. on 19th instand be guided to billets in Cité de L'ABBATIOR under arrangements to be made by me.
  2. Sections to M.28.c.8.2.
  1. Section to M.28.d.7.5. (Arranged by Mr. Shillito.)

The C.O. pf the 139th Coy will then issue orders to his sections Officers and the relief will proceed according to the table attached.

II

4. please acknowledge by bearer.

5. please advise by bearer if anything is not clear.

 18/4/17. 11.50.p.m. Sgd. H. Gilbert. Major" Commanding 73rd M.G.C.

III

TABLE issued with Relief Orders Night 19/20th April.

Teams No.	Guides one per team.	Outgoing limbers for 73 M.G.C.	Officer. i/c.	Remarks.
1. 2. 3.	To be at WHITE CHATEAU M.28.d. 7.8. at 8.30. p.m. 19th. April	Full limber at RED MILL at Midnight 19-20th April.	Lt. Whitworth.	White Chateau is the Support Batt H.Q.
4.	Ditto.	Ditto.	Lt. Tibbitt.	1 guide for 2/Lt. 3 outgoing teams will be at the RED Mill at 8.p.m. & 2 guides at Midnight to guide outgoing groups of 3 teams to COLONELS HOUSE by best route.
	2/Lt Shillito's 3 guns in CITE DE L'ABBATIOR.	Withdraw to full limber awaiting at RED MILL at 8.p.m.	2/Lt. Shillito will supervise the correct meeting of guides and relieving teams at WHITE CHATEAU. Further instructions later.	

N.B. 1. Guns 1=, 2, 3, 4, 5, 6. are the front line guns numbered from right to left.

2 . 139th Coy will take over from 73rd Coy 4 belt boxes per team Remainder will be brought out with outgoing teams.

IV

3. Guns and equipment in limbers will proceed to FOSSE I0. personnel will proceed to NOULETTE HUTS and report to C.S.M. In the event of better accommodation being found at FOSSE IO, the C.S.M will have a man waiting at COLONEL'S HOUSE to advise all outgoing personnel about this.

4. Mens packs will be put on the outgoing limbers at the Officers discretion.

5. Officers concerned must issue clear orders either personnaly or in writing to their N.C.O.s i/c teams re the actual relief of teams. In a case like this the handing over by the N.C.O's must be conscientiously done and all possible information about the disposition of our Infantry, enemy patrols and positions handed over. Officers must hand over to the relieving Officers all maps and information.

6. Sgt Evans will be at M.27.c.6.2. on outgoing route to receive from officers concerned reports of "complete relief."

7. It is most important that guides from teams should know the number of their gun.

OPERATION ORDER issued to Lt. Tibbitt. 73rd M.G.Coy.

Lt. Tibbitt.

The relief has been postponed for 24 hours. All previous orders hold good.

No rations are coming up to-night. Will you try and exist on Iron Rations until tomorrow.

I have seen Whitworth, re Sgt. Smith and Cpl. Follows.

19/4/17.
6.10.p.m.

Sgd. H. Gilbert, Major,
Commanding 73rd Machine Gun Company.

OPERATION ORDER issued to Lts. Croager and Bell.

Lt. Croager)
Lt. Bell.   )   73rd M. G. Coy.

I am sorry that my note of yesterday 3.p.m. didnot reach you before Sgt. Piggford set out to come here. Arrangements for our relief in the line on the night of 20/28st are now complete and we ought to get out "according to plan."

Re limbers to-night -please arrange that they do not get up earlier than the times I have given. The best spot to wait is, I think just past RED MILL.

Re our future moves:- It seems to me that the various move orders issued to us have been knocked on the head by the fact that our relief was a day late.

According to our move orders our moves were due as follows:-

From.	To.
21st. NOULETTE HUTS.	To be notified.
22nd. To be notified.	ESTREE BLANCHE.

I have since received a wire from TOMCAT (73rd Inf. Bde.) to say that we are due in MARLES LES MINES on the night 22/23rd April.

I take it we therefore need not move from PETIT SAINS until morning of the 22nd inst. This will give a complete day to reorganise a little and get ready for the move.

I enclose the two previous orders. I hope you clearly understand my statements.

As there were no rations sent to the line last night there must be plenty of food etc available for the men to have something afterrelief to-night when they come out. Please arrange this and let me know what the arrangements are.

Shillito's 5hree teams will be in about 9.30.p.m. and the remainder about 1.30.a.m.

The QMS should be arranging a supply of Bully Beef and Biscuits to make up a large number of deficient Iron Rations.

20/4/17.   Sgd. H. Gilbert, Major,
Noon.   Commanding 73rd Machine Gun Company.

Army Form C. 2118.

WAR DIARY
or
INTELLIGENCE SUMMARY.
(Erase heading not required.)

Vol 14

Confidential

War Diary
of
43rd Machine Gun Coy
for month of
May 1917

Army Form C. 2118.

WAR DIARY
or
INTELLIGENCE SUMMARY

(Erase heading not required.)

Instructions regarding War Diaries and Intelligence Summaries are contained in F. S. Regs., Part II. and the Staff Manual respectively. Title pages will be prepared in manuscript.

Place	Date	Hour	Summary of Events and Information	Remarks and references to Appendices
NOEUX LES MINES	1st MAY		2 N.C.Os proceeded to report to O.C. reinforcements ETAPLES (Kutty A.S.S. A 15742 and A/23232 LA A.A. C.R. No 16612/2930) in exchange for 2 N.C.Os arrived 29/4/17	C.E.L.G.
"	2 "		1 OR evacuated to C.C.S. 1 O.R joined the Company from the Base as reinforcement. Should have joined Coy on 22/4/15. Coy did routine work satisfactory.	C.E.L.G.
"	3 "		1 OR evacuated to C.C.S. arrived from Base as reinforcement on 2/5/17. Day spent in training. Reinforcements trained in use of revolver.	C.E.L.G.
"	4 "		1 OR admitted to hospital.	C.E.L.G.
"	5 "		After training in the morning preparations made for a move. Company ordered to move to HARUVRISRES. Carts to do are arrived 2.0pm marching good. No stragglers.	C.E.L.G.
HARUVRIERE	6		Day spent in reorganising. New clothing, equipment & arms. 1 OR admitted to hospital	C.E.L.G.
"	7		2/Lt G.7. FINCH joined Company as reinforcement from Base. Orders received by Brigade to attach a section to each Infantry Battln	C.E.L.G.

Army Form C. 2118.

WAR DIARY
or
INTELLIGENCE SUMMARY.
(Erase heading not required.)

Instructions regarding War Diaries and Intelligence Summaries are contained in F. S. Regs., Part II. and the Staff Manual respectively. Title pages will be prepared in manuscript.

Place	Date	Hour	Summary of Events and Information	Remarks and references to Appendices
LABRUYERE	8th May		1 OR discharged from hospital	CEG
	9 "		Training carried on by remaining men of company. Company had orders to proceed to L'ECLEME. Marching food no stragglers. Started 1.30 pm returned 4.10 pm.	CEG
L'ECLEME	10 "		Company moved from L'ECLEME to THIENNES. arrived 11.30 pm. Men set of by infantry in front stopping for dinner No stragglers 1 OR discharged from hospital after being evacuated sick.	CEG
THIENNES.	11 "		Company with detachments of Brigade inspected by Divisional Commander. State out of company very good.	CEG
"	12 "		2 OR admitted to hospital 1 OR evacuated to C.C.S. Orders to move to STEENVOORDE. Started 11.10 am arrived Esquin. Halted half way for 2½ hrs for dinner. Marching of company very fair considering heat. 2 stragglers.	CEG
STEENVOORDE	13 "		1 OR admitted to hospital & evacuated to C.C.S	CEG
"	14 "		1 OR " " " " " " "	CEG

2353 Wt. W2544/1454 700,000 5/15 D. D. & L. A.D.S.S./Forms/C. 2118.

WAR DIARY or INTELLIGENCE SUMMARY

Army Form C. 2118.

Place	Date	Hour	Summary of Events and Information	Remarks and references to Appendices
STEENVOORDE	14th May		Platoon to march to DEVONSHIRE CAMP. Starts march at P.45am. March very slow through our rough ground.	
DEVONSHIRE CP.	15"	"	O/R ordered to report to O.C. 220 M.G. Coy. to be transferred (authy. H.Q.s C.E. No. 14012/397. dt. 5/5/17 & 2nd Div. A.A. & Q.M.G. of B. A.F.37 dt. 4/5/17). 2/Lt. P.M. ANDREWS granted leave to UK to 25th inst.	C.B.G.
"	16 "	"	1 O.R. admitted to Hospital. Schemes of training carried on.	
"	17 "	"	1 O.R. admitted to hospital. Orders received from Division to the effect that Company to be attached to 47th Division for work. Three sections, consisting of 4 Officers & 63 O.R. sent up to the line to undertake work of making large emplacements. Proceeded to line at 5.0 pm.	C.B.G.
"	18 "	"	1 O.R. proceeded to report to O.C. 113th Army S Company on transfer for promotion to C.Q.M.S. (authy :– A.G. Ye. S/142.A. of. 5/5/17 and 2nd Div. A.A.& Q.M. No. A.93B of. 8/5/17.)	ShyL
"	19.		1 O.R. admitted to hospital	

WAR DIARY
INTELLIGENCE SUMMARY.

(Erase heading not required.)

Army Form C. 2118.

Place	Date	Hour	Summary of Events and Information	Remarks and references to Appendices
EVONSHIRE CP	20		2/Lieut SCOTT C.W. discharged from hospital. Lieut CROAGER and 2 O.R's proceeded to the Machine Gun School at Camieres. Lieut PHILPOTT T.A. and 2 O.R's returned to duty from Machine Gun School at CAMIERES.	
	21.		2 O.R's proceeded to 11th Army Rest Camp. 10 O.R's of the reserve section in rest, no details for mounts	
	22		Lieut PHILPOTT proceeded to the line to relieve 2/Lieut SHILLETO, who then took charge of No 3 Section. Lieut Libbett having returned to company to perform duties of 2nd in command vice Lieut CROAGER. On the night of the 22nd & 23rd two days rations were delivered to sections in the line to facilitate minimum work for transport. 1 O.R. granted leave to U.K. to 1st June 1917. 1 O.R. evacuated to C.C.S.	

WAR DIARY or INTELLIGENCE SUMMARY

Army Form C. 2118.

Place	Date	Hour	Summary of Events and Information	Remarks and references to Appendices
DEVONSHIRE C⁰	23rd		1 O.R. evacuated to C.C.S.	Plus.
	24th		2 OR! discharged from Hospital. 2/Lieut. ANDREWS. P.M. promoted Lieut. 1/3/17. Lieut. TIBBIT. E.M. admitted to Hospital	Plus.
	25th		1 O.R. proceeded to ADEELE for course of map Reading. Lieut. SCOTT. C.W. admitted to Hospital Lieut. WHITWORTH. W.M. awarded MILITARY CROSS.	Plus.
	26th		1 O.R. wounded in action. 3 OR's. admitted to Hospital. Lieut. ANDREWS. P.M. returned to duty from leave to U.K.	Plus.
	27th		1 O.R. evacuated. Lieut. TIBBITT. E.M. mentioned in dispatches 26/5/17. Lieut. ANDREWS. P.M. took up duty of 2nd in Command. Work done by sections in the line from the 17th onwards had consisted of carrying up ammunition and making Battery Emery Position.	Plus. Plus.

WAR DIARY
or
INTELLIGENCE SUMMARY.

(Erase heading not required.)

Army Form C. 2118.

Place	Date	Hour	Summary of Events and Information	Remarks and references to Appendices
DEVONSHIRE Camp.	28th.		1 O.R. evacuated to C.C.S.	Plea.
"	29th		1 O.R. reported missing. He was last seen on the morning of the 27th. 2/Lieut. Scott. C.W. returned to duty from Hospital. 1.O.R. returned to duty from Hospital. Orders to march to No 25 Camp. ZEVECOTEN.	Plea.
25 Camp. ZEVECOTEN.	30th.		Company moved off at 2.0. p.m. arriving at 3.30 p.m. Training in the use of the Yukon Pack.	Plea.
	31st		10 Tents were drawn from the Area Commandant to accomodate the remainder of the Company when relief takes place.	Plea.

Lieut Major
Commanding 3rd Coy.

Army Form C. 2118.

WAR DIARY

~~INTELLIGENCE SUMMARY~~

(Erase heading not required.)

Instructions regarding War Diaries and Intelligence Summaries are contained in F. S. Regs., Part II. and the Staff Manual respectively. Title pages will be prepared in manuscript.

Place	Date	Hour	Summary of Events and Information	Remarks and references to Appendices

General

93rd Machine Gun Company

For the month of

June 1917

WAR DIARY or INTELLIGENCE SUMMARY

Army Form C. 2118.

Place	Date	Hour	Summary of Events and Information	Remarks and references to Appendices
ZEVECOTEN.	1/6/17		1 O.R. discharged from Hospital. Lieut. E.S. MILLER proceeded to report to the Commandant Engineer Training Centre NEWARK - Auth: G.H.Q. A/25399 27/5/17. 24th Div'l A.A. + Q.M.G. A162/. 30/5/17. 3 Sections came out of the line and proceeded to Company H.Q. arriving there at 3 A.M.	Plus.
"	2/6/17		Lieut. WHITWORTH W.M. admitted to Hospital. 1 O.R. admitted to Hospital.	ALLO. Plus.
"	3/6/17		Company work - equipping and training.	
"	4/6/17		1 O.R. discharged from Hospital.	Plus.
"	5/6/17		2 Officers, with skeleton teams took up BARRAGE positions in Fort of VOORMEZEELE at 10.0. P.M. 16 guns went up as well. 4 Officers and remainder of team proceeded to barrage position at 8.45. P.M.	Mus.
"	6/6/17		18 O.R's attached to the Company proceeded to the Transit 8. U.S. P.M.	Mus.

WAR DIARY or INTELLIGENCE SUMMARY

Army Form C. 2118.

Place	Date	Hour	Summary of Events and Information	Remarks and references to Appendices
OUDERDOM	7/6/17		Attack on the MESSINES - WYTSCHAETE ridge began with intense barrage artillery barrage at 3.10 a.m. The 16 guns of the Company opened with barrage fire and supported the attack by the 41st Div on the BLUE and BLACK line. 1 Officer and 7 men proceeded to Brigade H.Q. at SUFFOLK MANOR Farm when intense shell fire was made established. 1 Officer and remainder of Company including transport moved to OTTAWA CAMP (OUDERDOM) where they established new H.Q. By 12 midday the BLUE and BLACK lines were secured. The 2nd M.G. Company joined the 73rd I.B. and in the attack against the green line. 8 guns were attached to the Battalion, 2 in support and 4 in reserve. At 1 o'clock I.H.Q. moved forward with Brigade H.Q. to CONVENT LANE TRENCH, where their permanent H.Q. were established.	

WAR DIARY
or
INTELLIGENCE SUMMARY.

(Erase heading not required.)

Army Form C. 2118.

Place	Date	Hour	Summary of Events and Information	Remarks and references to Appendices
OUDERDOM	7/6/17		By 4 o'clock, the GREEN LINE had been captured and the ground beyond this had been placed in position covering the front line which the Infantry consolidated. T.H.Q. moved forward, taking up permanent H.Q. in the DAMM STRASSE. 2 Guns in support were attached to the 9th Royal Sussex. The 4 Guns in support were placed in donjes position in the DAMM STRASSE. The enemy made no counter attack during the night, and the night passed quietly. 2 ORs killed in action. 2 ORs wounded in action. 1 OR returned from leave. 2 ORs returned to duty from rest camp. Telephonic communication established between T.M.Q. and I.M.Q. Work of consolidation continued throughout the day. Heavy enemy counter attack was launched	Plan.
"	8/6/17			

WAR DIARY or INTELLIGENCE SUMMARY

Army Form C. 2118.

Place	Date	Hour	Summary of Events and Information	Remarks and references to Appendices
OVDERDOM	8/6/17		against the whole new front at 7 o'clock. This was broken up and failed to materialize owing to artillery and machine gun fire. The barrage from our artillery & Stokes field 6000 rounds. By midnight the artillery fire died down and the remainder of the night passed quietly. 1 OR. admitted to Hospital. 1 OR. reported missing. The day passed quietly. Lieut. CROFGER and 3 ORs. returned to duty from CAMIERES. Lieut. CROFGER took over the duties of 2nd in Command. Lieut. ANDREWS proceeded to H.Q. 2/Lieut. SCOTT admitted to Hospital. 1 OR. " " 5 ORs killed in action	Na.
"	9/6/17			

WAR DIARY
or
INTELLIGENCE SUMMARY.
(Erase heading not required.)

Army Form C. 2118.

Place	Date	Hour	Summary of Events and Information	Remarks and references to Appendices
GUDEROM	9/6/17		2 O.Rs. wounded in action. 1 O.R. missing believed in hospital. Lieut ANDREWS took over the 2 guns which were attached to 13th Middlesex	M.C.
	10/6/17		in RAVINE WOOD. 1 O.R. wounded in action	Elst.
			1 O.R. granted leave to U.K. Lieut. Hodges proceeded to Divisional H.Q. to relieve Major GILBERT. 2 O.R's wounded in action.	
	11/6/17		Major GILBERT return to intermediate Company H.Q. On the night 12th/13th the Company was relieved by 124th M.G. Company Relief completed by 3 a.m. Guns dumped at SGT MEZEELE.	Elst.
	12/6/17		1 O.R. admitted to hospital 1 O.R. exchanged from hospital 1 O.R's reinforcements joined from Base.	Elst.
	13/6/17		Relieved teams proceeded to OTTAWA CAMP. 1 O.R. admitted to hospital	Elst.

WAR DIARY
or
INTELLIGENCE SUMMARY.
(Erase heading not required.)

Army Form C. 2118.

Place	Date	Hour	Summary of Events and Information	Remarks and references to Appendices
MICMAC CAMP	14/4/17		Company moved to MICMAC CAMP. 2 O.R.'s discharged from hospital. 8 O.R. reinforcements joined from Base.	Appx 1
	15/4/17		Company relieved 19 A.G Company in the "HILL 60" Sector on the night of the 15-16/17. Although shelling was heavy we sustained no casualties. Lt Whitworth discharged from hospital.	Appx
	16/4/17		3 O.R.'s discharged from hospital. 1 O.R. killed in action. 1 O.R. wounded in action.	Appx
	17/4/17		Lieut CROZIER went on leave to U.K., Lieut ANDREWS took over the duties of 2 in command. General Situation remained unchanged, shelling increased in the neighbourhood of the CATERPILLAR & S.P.9. 2 O.R.'s admitted to hospital. 1 O.R. killed in action	Appx

WAR DIARY
or
INTELLIGENCE SUMMARY.
(Erase heading not required.)

Army Form C. 2118.

Instructions regarding War Diaries and Intelligence Summaries are contained in F. S. Regs., Part II. and the Staff Manual respectively. Title pages will be prepared in manuscript.

Place	Date	Hour	Summary of Events and Information	Remarks and references to Appendices
MICMAC CAMP	17/6/17		2 O.R.'s wounded in action	Sht I.
	18/6/17		2/Lieut. SHILLITO and 2 teams proceeded to take IMPERIAL SUPPORT & take up positions covering the ground in rear of BATTLE WOOD. Major GILBERT proceeded from Rear H.Q. to take up his headquarters in S.P.9. Owing to heavy shelling forward Company H.Q. moved into S.P.9. 2 O.R.'s admitted to hospital. 2 O.R.'s proceeded to 2nd ARMY Rest Camp. Sgt. EVANS & Corpl. DOUGHTY awarded the Military Medal.	Sht I.
	19/6/17		2/Lieut. FINCH with 1 team proceeded from Rear Company H.Q. to relieve teams in the line. 2/Lieut. FINCH relieved Lt. PHILPOTT at TRIANGULAR BLUFF who returned to Transport Lines and took over the duties of O.C. Details. 2/Lieut. SHILLITO relieved 2/Lieut. GOURLAY at the CATERPILLAR who returned to Forward Company H.Q. 3 O.R.'s admitted to hospital	Sht I.

Army Form C. 2118.

WAR DIARY
or
INTELLIGENCE SUMMARY.
(Erase heading not required.)

Instructions regarding War Diaries and Intelligence Summaries are contained in F. S. Regs., Part II. and the Staff Manual respectively. Title pages will be prepared in manuscript.

Place	Date	Hour	Summary of Events and Information	Remarks and references to Appendices.
MICMAC CAMP	19/6/17		1 O.R. wounded in action	Ely
	20/6/17		The relief begun on the previous evening, was completed without casualties. 2 O.R.'s admitted to hospital. Lieut WHITWORTH + servant admitted to hospital. 2 O.R.'s discharged from hospital. 1 O.R. granted leave to U.K.	Ely
	21/6/17		The forward company of 9 moved from S.P.9. to the "BLUFF". Intermittent shelling throughout the day and night. Lieut TIBBITT discharged from hospital and posted to R.E. Dept rejoined the company.	Ely
	22/6/17		9 O.R. reinforcements joined the Company from Base Depot. 2 guns placed in position in INSULT TRENCH, the guns were reported in position by 6.0 p.m. 2 guns were mounted on the SPOIL BANK Storage. Low flying hostile aircraft. 2 O.R's returns from leave D.U.R.	Ely

WAR DIARY
or
INTELLIGENCE SUMMARY
(Erase heading not required.)

Army Form C. 2118.

Place	Date	Hour	Summary of Events and Information	Remarks and references to Appendices
MICMAC CAMP	23/6/17		The 73rd M.G.Coy was billeted in the lines of the 72nd M.G.Coy.	
"	24/6/17	1.0.R.	granted leave to U.K.	
		1.O.R.	evacuated to C.C.S.	
		2/Lt. CARTER. E.O	joined the Company from the base.	Plum
			The relief of the Company was reported complete by 4.30 am without casualties. Advanced teams proceeded to relieve Coys.	
			1 O.R. admitted to hospital and evacuated to C.C.S.	
			Lieut. Tibbit resumed the duties of 2/i/c.	Plum
"	25/6/17		Cleaning up and refitting. 2/Lt. PHILPOTT with a portion of the transport left for the II Army Rest Area.	Plum
"	26/6/17		Lieut. ANDREWS and 2/Lt. GOURLAY left at 8.30 am to arrange for billets at the new area. M.C. Staff arrangements.	
			10. R. evacuated to C.C.S.	Plum
"	27/6/17		Company and remainder of transport left McMichae Camp and entrained for new rest area.	

Army Form C. 2118.

WAR DIARY
or
INTELLIGENCE SUMMARY

(Erase heading not required.)

Instructions regarding War Diaries and Intelligence Summaries are contained in F. S. Regs., Part II. and the Staff Manual respectively. Title pages will be prepared in manuscript.

Place	Date	Hour	Summary of Events and Information	Remarks and references to Appendices
RAYENGHEM	27/6/17		The Company arrived in their billets at 9.30 p.m. 1 O.R. evacuated to CCS.	Nil
"	28/6/17		Cleaning and refitting. P.T. and Squad drill for reinforcement.	Nil
"	29/6/17		Unloading timber and equipment. Training for reinforcement. Lieut T. Tibbitt granted leave to U.K. Lieut Andrews took up the duties of 2/I/c. 2/Lt. PHILPOTT promoted Lieut. 1/5/17. Sgt. DISNEY H. awarded D.C.M.	
"	30/6/17		Nil	Nil

Signed,
MAJOR
COMMANDING ___ M.G. COY.
MACHINE GUN CORPS.

Army Form C. 2118.

WAR DIARY
or
INTELLIGENCE SUMMARY.
(Erase heading not required.)

74 Bre

Vol 16

Instructions regarding War Diaries and Intelligence Summaries are contained in F. S. Regs., Part II. and the Staff Manual respectively. Title pages will be prepared in manuscript.

Place	Date	Hour	Summary of Events and Information	Remarks and references to Appendices
Peronne			War Diary of 74th Machine Gun Company for month of July 1917	

WAR DIARY
or
INTELLIGENCE SUMMARY.

(Erase heading not required.)

Army Form C. 2118.

Instructions regarding War Diaries and Intelligence Summaries are contained in F. S. Regs., Part II. and the Staff Manual respectively. Title pages will be prepared in manuscript.

Place	Date	Hour	Summary of Events and Information	Remarks and references to Appendices
BAYENGHEM	1/2/17		Church Parade at 11.0 am.	
			Lieut. WOOD. G.W.H. joined the Company on retirement from the Base.	MA
"	2/7/17		2nd M/f/Co and L.T.M. Batty. Spots at 2.15 pm.	
			Lieut. CROSSER. returned from leave.	
			2/Lt. SCOTT. C.W. discharged from Hospital and rejoined the Company.	PUA
			1.O.R discharged from Hosp. W.	
"	3/7/17		Training.	PUA
			2. O.R.s granted leave to U.K. with ration allowance.	
"	4/7/17		Continued training.	
			1. O.R. proceeded to II Army Gas School to undergo a course.	
"	5/7/17		1. O.R. return from leave.	PUA
	6/7/17		Training continued	PUA
			also	PUA

WAR DIARY
INTELLIGENCE SUMMARY.
(Erase heading not required.)

Army Form C. 2118.

Place	Date	Hour	Summary of Events and Information	Remarks and references to Appendices
BRYENGHEM	7/7/17		Training.	
			2 O.Rs. returned from leave to U.K.	
			Major GILBERT M.C. + 20 Rs. proceeded to N.B. 24th DIV.	plus.
	8/7/17		Training.	
			Lieut. T.H.D. DELL granted leave to U.K.	plus.
	9th		Company paraded at 6.15 A.M. and proceeded to LE WAST	
			on the way to the coast, arriving there 1.0. P.M.	
			3 O.Rs. joined the Company from the base as Reinforcements.	plus.
LE WAST.	10/7/17		Company paraded 9.0 A.M. and proceeded to BAYENGHEM	
			on its way back from the coast, arriving at 3.0 P.M.	
			Major GILBERT M.E. appointed P.M.G.O.	
			Auth:- GRHQ No O.B. 607 d/- 17/6/17 and 24th Div.	
			A/2386. d/- 10/7/17.	
BAYENGHEM	11/7/17		Company continued it training.	plus.
			1 O.R. admitted to Hosp. Cl.	plus.

WAR DIARY
or
INTELLIGENCE SUMMARY.
(Erase heading not required.)

Army Form C. 2118.

Place	Date	Hour	Summary of Events and Information	Remarks and references to Appendices
BAYENGHEM	12/7/17		Training 3 sub-sections attached to 2/Kensnt and 2/Northant trained in the evening with the Battalion.	
			1.O.R. rejoined the company.	Plus.
"	13/7/17		Training continued Range firing sub-section trained with Battalion	Plus
"	14/7/17		Training in the morning, 73rd I.B. Sports on the afternoon.	Plus
"	15/7/17		Church Parade at 11.0 a.m.	Plus
			1.O.R. wounded (self-inflicted)	Plus.
"	16/7/17		Sub-section trained to 4th Battalion remainder trained in bomb work for forth-coming operations.	
			1.O.R. proceeded to report to O.C. Transportation troops CALAIS. Auth. D.A.G. C.R. no 18745/2-17/17) A dated 11/7/17.	
			LIEUT TIBBOTT returned from leave, K.U.C.	Plus
			1.O.R. returned from leave K.U.C.	
			1.O.R. discharged from Hospital.	k

WAR DIARY
or
~~INTELLIGENCE SUMMARY.~~

(Erase heading not required.)

Army Form C. 2118.

Place	Date	Hour	Summary of Events and Information	Remarks and references to Appendices
BAYENGHEM	17/7/17		Training. Barrage Teams 2nd practice barrage range. Sub-section. Tennis with Battalion	
			2. O.R.s admitted to Hospital.	Plus
	18/7/17		Company paraded 3.0 a.m. and marched from BAYENGHEM to LE NIEPPE arriving at the latter place at 10.0 A.M. The condition of the men was GP and there were no stragglers.	
			1 O.R. evacuated to C.C.S.	Plus
LE NIEPPE	19/7/17		Company paraded 5.0 P.M. and marched to CAESTRE where they went billeted in the Barns for the night.	
			1. O.R. evacuated and admitted to Hospital and evacuated to C.C.S.	Plus
CAESTRE.	20/7/17		Company paraded 8.0 A.M. and marched to EEKE.	Plus
EEKE.	21/7/17	"	6.0 A.M. and marched to PENINGHSLST STAGING AREA. On route they were joined by a Section of the 17th M.G. Coy. Company arrived 11.0 a.m. 24th CRUCKWELL E.E. joined the Company as a reinforcement from the base	Plus

WAR DIARY
INTELLIGENCE SUMMARY

Army Form C. 2118.

Place	Date	Hour	Summary of Events and Information	Remarks and references to Appendices
RENINGHELST	22/7/17		Lts. CROAGER, ANDREWS, & PHILPOT went to see the O.C. by the Maj. Gen. in Lower Wood Tramway Nick. 6 Guns must. 2/Lt WOOD, 2/Lt. SCOTT and FINCH observed afrem of the Bgt. M.G/Cos. Relief reported complet 10 am.	
			1. O.R. discharged from Hospital.	Appx
			1. O.R. admitted to Hospital.	
			Company paraded at 6 P.M. and marched to MICMAC Camp.	Appx.
MICMAC	23/7/17		Lt Philpot & 2/Lt Gordon went up to line to reconnoitre battery positions.	
			1. O.R. discharged from Hosp. Tal.	
			3 O.Rs. joined the Company as reinforcements from the Base	
			Lt. WENTWORTH M.M. was reported departing for England (P.R.C list) and is struck off the Strength accordingly.	Appx.
	24/7/17		2/Lt. FINCH and one team returned from MOUNT SORREL.	
"			2/Lt. SCOTT and on team went forward to MOUNT SORREL	
			1. O.R. discharged from Hosp. Tal.	

WAR DIARY
INTELLIGENCE SUMMARY

(Erase heading not required.)

Army Form C. 2118.

Place	Date	Hour	Summary of Events and Information	Remarks and references to Appendices
MICHIEL C.	24/7/17		Casualties:— 3 O.Rs. Killed in action. 3 O.Rs. wounded in action.	Nil.
"	25/7/17		1 team proceeded to MONTSIRREL without the afternoon.	Nil.
"	26/7/17		2/Lt. Finch returned to Camp. Lt. Bell returned from leave.	Nil.
"	27/7/17		2/Lt. CRACKNELL proceeded to D. Battery Position.	Nil.
"	28/7/17		Lt. Wood came down to Camp from D. Battery Position. 1 O.R. proceeded to a course of instruction at CAMIERS. 2 guns were sent out to D. Battery Position.	Nil.
"	29/7/17		Lieut. CROZIER. appointed Acting Captain. 3000 rounds fired during the night.	
"	30/7/17		1 O.R. discharged from Hosp. Cat. 2/Lt. Stubbs and 2 teams proceeded to Mount Sorrel to join 2nd LEINSTERS.	Nil.
"	30/7/17		2/Lt. FINCH and 2 teams proceeded to Camerlin Tunnels to join 7th NORTHANTS.	

WAR DIARY
INTELLIGENCE SUMMARY.
(Erase heading not required.)

Army Form C. 2118.

Place	Date	Hour	Summary of Events and Information	Remarks and references to Appendices
MICMAC	30/7/17		2/Lt. Blower and 1 team proceeded to Mount Sorel to join 2 nd Leinsters. Captain Craggs proceeded to Company HQ in LARCH WOOD. Lieut Andrew proceeded to D Battery position. 2/Lt. Carter and 2 teams proceeded from 13th Middlesex in LARCH WOOD. 26 ORs. were attached to the Company 13 from 13th Middlesex and 13 from 2nd Northants.	
"	31/7/17		At 3.50 a.m. the attack on the Blue line commenced. The machine gun barrage opened at zero with the artillery. Teams attached to battalions went forward with them at zero. 2/Lt Shillito wounded. 2 ORs. killed in action. 14 ORs. wounded in action.	M.G.

A.M.Bridgworth Lt
for Captain
Commanding 143 M.G. Coy.

Army Form C. 2118.

WAR DIARY

INTELLIGENCE SUMMARY

(Erase heading not required.)

96/17

143rd. Machine Gun Company

for the month of

August 1917.

Army Form C. 2118.

WAR DIARY
or
INTELLIGENCE SUMMARY.
(Erase heading not required.)

Instructions regarding War Diaries and Intelligence Summaries are contained in F. S. Regs., Part II. and the Staff Manual respectively. Title pages will be prepared in manuscript.

Place	Date	Hour	Summary of Events and Information	Remarks and references to Appendices
MICMAC CAMP	1/8/17		2/Lt. Finch and 2 Teams met returned to CHIPPA TUNNELS.	nil.
"	2/8/17		2/Lt. Blower and 1 Team returned to Camp. 2/Lt. CARTER admitted to Hospital accompanied by his servant. 1 O.R. discharged from Hospital.	nil.
"	3/8/17		2/Lt. WOOD and 2 Teams proceeded to position forward of Mount Sorrel support 13th Brigade. 1 O.R. admitted and evacuated to C.C.S.	nil.
"	4/8/17		Lt. PHILPOTT and 4 Teams proceeded to LARCH WOOD. 1 O.R. admitted to Hospital.	nil.
"	5/8/17		Lt. PHILPOTT and 2 Teams proceeded to front line position on left of SHREWSBURY FOREST support 9 K. Scott. 2/Lt. CRACKNELL and 2 Teams proceeded to position in front of HEDGE STR. TUNNELS. Lt. WOOD relieved by 2 gun's of 191st Company.	

WAR DIARY
INTELLIGENCE SUMMARY.
(Erase heading not required.)

Army Form C. 2118.

Place	Date	Hour	Summary of Events and Information	Remarks and references to Appendices
Meerut	1/8/17		Lt. ANDREWS and 2/Lt. GORELAY with 4 teams relieved by "G" Company and proceeded to M.C.M.P.C. camp. 2/Lt. Turnbull returned to BASE.	
			1 O.R. rejoined from hospital	
			3 O.Rs. admitted to hospital	follow
			Lieut. BENNETT G.S.M. joined the Company from the BASE as 2/in command.	MM
Marseilles	6-8-17		Team Reveilly Uhens occupied in cleaning the shipping. 2nd Lt. FINCH admitted to hospital. 3 O.R.s admitted to hospital.	P.M.B.
"	7.8.17		27 O.R's joined Re-inforcements from the Base. Details removed to M Camp Disturbance	P.M.B.
M. Camp Disturbance	8-8-17		Capt. Senger C.E.R. and 2/Lt. Philpott & Tackwell with remainder of Company were relieved in the this by 4th Coy. Relief Complete by 7.35 am.	P.M.B.
"	9.8.17		Company Engaged in refilling and reorganizing. 2 O.R's evacuated to C.C.S.	P.M.B.
"	10.8.17		Company proceeded to New Camp Dickeland. C.S.M. Simpson proceeded to join 1st Br. H.A.C. previous to returning to England on his commission	P.M.B.

WAR DIARY or INTELLIGENCE SUMMARY.

(Erase heading not required.)

Army Form C. 2118.

Instructions regarding War Diaries and Intelligence Summaries are contained in F. S. Regs., Part II. and the Staff Manual respectively. Title pages will be prepared in manuscript.

Place	Date	Hour	Summary of Events and Information	Remarks and references to Appendices
M Camp Dickebusch	11.8.17		Company proceeded to the line in afternoon, taking over Coy positions from 7th Company and placing two extra guns in the vicinity of Ridge St Quentin in the line. Mounted for A.A purposes. Two positions not relieved till 10.30 p.m. owing. Details to bivouac. 1 O.R. rejoined from hospital. 1 O.R. evacuated.	R.M.S.
Line	12.8.17		1 O.R. wounded. 1 O.R. discharged from hospital. 1 O.R. evacuated.	R.M.S.
"	13.8.17		Quiet day. Nothing to report. 3 O.R.'s admitted to hospital.	R.M.S.
"	14.8.17		Brought two more teams up to relieve two teams of 191st Coy in front line.	R.M.S.
			Relief completed. Further O.R's brought up for carrying purposes. 1 O.R. killed. 1 O.R. danged. 1 O.R. evacuated sick.	R.M.S.
	15.8.17		Orders received to concentrate in support of 38th Divn. Three men [?] attack a...	
			The 88th 14 guns of company to be used. Guns brought up from camp to available men employed carrying them to S.A.A. to Battery position. It brothers retired to join 195th Coy as escort in command that returned to [?]	
			out with 88th Sunday a Battery Commander. Guns laid to range. Co.	
			for Co. could be clear in shot item at disposal. 12 teams in line. Relieved Coy 72nd Coy & proceeded to vicinity of Battery positions. Relief complete	R.M.S.
			Coy 12.30 A.m.	

Army Form C. 2118.

WAR DIARY
or
INTELLIGENCE SUMMARY.
(Erase heading not required.)

Instructions regarding War Diaries and Intelligence Summaries are contained in F. S. Regs., Part II. and the Staff Manual respectively. Title pages will be prepared in manuscript.

Place	Date	Hour	Summary of Events and Information	Remarks and references to Appendices
Line	16.8.17		Attack by 56th Div. Commenced 4.45 a.m. Owing to lack of time for preparation	
			Exercise Shell fire & soft nature of ground where Tattoos from Coy falling down.	
			Artillery barrage of machine guns to carry on Relief. Few rounds fired. Coy.	
			remained in position all day. All Tanks Evacuated.	Maj.
Line	17.8.17		Company received orders to withdraw. Tattoos fell forward to Trichon Camp	Maj.B
Trichon	18.8.17		Company employed cleaning up & Tanks issued with clothing per 2C.S.P. distance from tank camp 3 O.R. admitted to hospital.	Maj.B.
Trichon	19.8.17		Bell filling, Checking Guns + Equipment Company proceeded in Lorries to	
			M. Camp Dickebusch. 3 O.R.'s admitted to hospital.	S.M.B.
M. Camp Dickebusch	20.8.17		Bell filling. Some of Spare parts Received machine Rollers received their	
			16 guns turned Complete in an attack by 14th Division n on Sept 6	
			guns to form as Tattoos & 4 Guns with 2 of the 191st Coy to form a	
			Second for Savage Kings. 7 O.R.'s admitted to hospital. Reinforcements - O.R.'s 3.	S.M.B.
Dickebusch	21.8.17		Morning occupied by Cleaning & Tracing units into Schemes Equipment	
			for Savage Caps Barrage, & After Sunday Blown proceeded to the Line to	
			Mark out Tattoo positions. It closed with 16 teams Every available Spare	
			Man for Carrying purposes proceeded to Line in the Evening. All Equipment	

WAR DIARY
or
INTELLIGENCE SUMMARY.
(Erase heading not required.)

Army Form C. 2118.

Instructions regarding War Diaries and Intelligence Summaries are contained in F. S. Regs., Part II. and the Staff Manual respectively. Title pages will be prepared in manuscript.

Place	Date	Hour	Summary of Events and Information	Remarks and references to Appendices
Line	22.8.17		was taken to Falling position at once. 7 O.R. accommodated in Ranch. Scout Patrols from the Regt. 8 O.R's admitted to Hospital. 6 O.R's evacuated. 1 O.R rejoined Regiment. Barrage fired from vicinity of Hedge Sr. Summit in cooperation with operation by 14th Div. on our left. Zero hour was 7.30. Fire was opened promptly maintained for one hour. Nearly 40,000 rounds were fired. Guns were withdrawn at 11.30. Main was accommodated at Ranch level. A Philpott & 4 O.R. admitted to Hospital; 1 O.R evacuated to positions in Camp.	Stars. Stars. Stars.
Line	23.8.17		Team remained in Ranch level all day until enemy W.R. position in this Team taken over from 17th Coy. to Guns were put into the line 2 in reserve. Hedge Sr. and 4 in course of changes. Relief comp'd about 3.20 a.m. Major A Philpott and 3 O.R's admitted to Hospital. Major A Pollard was wounded on Aug. 20th. Stabs. Div. on left. Sgt Murphy from E.Rees left position	Stabs.
Line	24.8.17		Enemy Combt. attacked 14th Div. on Left. Sgt Murphy from E.Rees left position Opened fire with good effect at close range. 1 O.R evacuated to C.C.S.	Stars.
Line	25.8.17		Quiet day. Nothing to report. 3 O.R's admitted to Hospital. 1 O.R evacuated to C.C.S.	Stars.
Line	26.8.17		Opp. Blows from No. 5 position disposed Enemy patrol. We also got into a Good target at about 2000 range. Good effect was observed. 6 O.R's admitted to Hospital. 1 O.R committed.	Stars.
Line	27.8.17		Company relieved in the line by 72nd Coy. Relief complete by 11.35 pm. 1 O.R wounded. 1 O.R evacuated to C.C.S. Relief company proceeded to Vierman Camp. 1 O.R wounded. 1 O.R evacuated from Hospital. 8 O.R's discharged from Hospital.	Stars.

M6915 Wt. W11422/M1160 350,000 12/16 D.D. & L. Forms/C./2118/14.

WAR DIARY
or
INTELLIGENCE SUMMARY.
(Erase heading not required.)

Army Form C. 2118.

Place	Date	Hour	Summary of Events and Information	Remarks and references to Appendices
Muhrar	28.9.17		Company employed cleaning up & tidying. Buried half Kit. 1 OR Evacuated to C.C.S. 5 OR discharged from Hospital.	GMB.
"	29.9.17		Shooting from shelter & throwing gun Grenades & rifle grenades that taken over in line by relieving Coy. 2/Lt Gundry & Cpl Dorothy proceeded to Ramleh for M.G. Course. 2 OR's admitted to Hospital. 4 OR's discharged from Hospital. 4 OR's reported as reinforcement. 2 OR's Evacuated to C.C.S.	GMB. GMB.
"	30.9.17		Company training. 4 OR's admitted to Hospital. 2 OR's discharged from Hosp.	GMB.
"	31.9.17		Company training. Company proceeded to Railway Camp Dutschach in New Training. Taking over from 17th M.G. Coy who proceeded to this. 1 OR admitted. 1 OR discharged from Hospital. 2 OR's Evacuated to C.C.S.	GMB.

Clithorpe Captain

Army Form C. 2118.

WAR DIARY
INTELLIGENCE SUMMARY
(Erase heading not required.)

Vol / 8

Secret.

43rd Machine Gun Company
for the month of
September 1917.

WAR DIARY or INTELLIGENCE SUMMARY

Army Form C. 2118.

Place	Date	Hour	Summary of Events and Information	Remarks and references to Appendices
Dernancourt	1-9-17		Company training. 9 O.R's admitted to Hospital. 2/Lt R.R. Rolan joined the Coy from the Base & Reinforcements.	Offrs.
"	2-9-17		1 O.R. Discharged. Voluntary Church parade for all Denominations. Company engaged in Sand-bagging. Capt. Barger & 2/Lt Bennett proceeded to line on Reconnaissance near Thus. 4 O.R's admtd. to Hospital. 2 O.R's discharged.	Offrs.
"	3-9-17		Company proceeded to line in relief of Northern R.L. taking over 5 positions from 7th M.G. Company. 7th M.G. Company, and four positions from 6th M.G. Company. Gun Crews. Additional line in reserve in Hedge St. Tunnels. 5 O.R's admitted to Hosp. 1 O.R discharged.	Offrs.
line	4-9-17		Owing to the Brigade taking over part of the line two different Brigades the Coy relief could not be reported complete till 12 pm. 4 O.R's Evacuated to C.C.S.	Offrs.
"	5-9-17		Company H.Q. being in the 2nd Divisional Area, orders were received to evacuate. This was done & H.Q. moved to No 1 Sec. Evacuate when new H.Q. was found.	
"	6-9-17		Position in the front line. 4 O.R's Evacuated to C.C.S. Company received orders to prepare a falling position. Group S.A.A. dump Etc. for forthcoming operation by 23rd Division. Work was commenced on this. Superised by 2/Lt Blows. 1 O.R Discharged Hospital. 3 O.R's formed for Love.	Gas. Offrs.
"	7-9-17		Work for falling position proceeded with. Assisted by Carrying Parties from 13th Man.R. Company Relieved during afternoon & evening by 72nd M.S.	

A6945 Wt. W14422/M1160 350,000 12/16 D.D. & L. Form/C/2118/14.

Army Form C. 2118.

WAR DIARY
or
INTELLIGENCE SUMMARY.
(Erase heading not required.)

Instructions regarding War Diaries and Intelligence Summaries are contained in F. S. Regs., Part II. and the Staff Manual respectively. Title pages will be prepared in manuscript.

Place	Date	Hour	Summary of Events and Information	Remarks and references to Appendices
Micmac			Company Relief completed by about midnight. On relief, the Company proceeded to its old quarters in MICMAC CAMP. 7 OR's admitted to Hosp. 2 OR's discharged	Appx.
	8-9-17		Company engaged resting & cleaning up. 11 Civno Exports & taken over in the line. 2 OR's discharged from Hosp.	Appx.
"	9-9-17		From 72nd Coy, & replaced those handed over in the line. 2 OR's discharged from Hosp. Working Party of 40 men from 19th M.C. Coy put at the disposal of 73rd Coy for completing Preparations for Barrage. 4 OR's discharged from Hospital.	Appx.
"	10-9-17		2nd Lt Rogers with two Sections & working party from 19th Coy took 140 Boxes of S.A.A. to Battery position. In the evening 2nd Lt B Shore & 30 men of the Coy proceeded to Battery position & worked all night making shell slits for self filling Party. 2nd Lt Blaser returned at dawn + 2nd Lt Blaser returned at dawn. Remaining at Battery position to Sept Even tead further work by 19th Coy. Kit Inspection held. 4 OR's granted leave to U.K. 2 OR's admitted to Hospital. 3 OR's discharged. 4 OR's proceeded to Base Depot.	Appx.
"	11-9-17		Company engaged cleaning timber & preparing for move to Brewery Camp Dickebusch	Appx.

WAR DIARY
or
INTELLIGENCE SUMMARY.
(Erase heading not required.)

Army Form C. 2118.

Place	Date	Hour	Summary of Events and Information	Remarks and references to Appendices
Dickebusch	12-9-17		Carrying party of 30 M.E. took 140,000 rounds S.A.A. to dump at HdQs. S.M. In view of forthcoming operations 2 O.R's admitted to C.C.S. 2 O.R's evacuated for fungus foot.	Maj. B.
"	13-9-17		180,000 rounds S.A.A. carried to dump. 2 Coy under order of Coy Bugler.	Maj. B.
"			Preparations for moving to Reserve. 1 O.R. admitted. 3 O.R's discharged. 1 O.R. evacuated to C.C.S. Wounded from fatigue.	Maj. B.
"	14-9-17		Coy paraded at 2 pm. Proceeded by French route to WESTOUTRE, where Camp was taken over for one night.	Maj. B.
WESTOUTRE	16-9-17		Company proceeded by m.tr. bus to BERGUIN over 9 went via LE VERRIER.	Maj. B.
BERGUIN	16-9-17		Company restat. 3 O.R's discharged. 1 O.R. reported sick. Cav. 4 O.R's Ratified Leave E.C.W.	Maj. B.
"	17-9-17		Company training. 1 O.R's return from sick leave to U.K. Company inspected by his protestant Major Gen...	Maj. B.
"	18-9-17		Company training. 1 O.R. discharged from Hospital. 1 O.R. evacuated to C.C.S.	Maj. B.
"	19-9-17		Company training.	Maj. B.
"	20-9-17		Practice man handling timbers. Coy paraded at 11:30 to march to BAILLEUL. Stables for entraining.	Maj. B.
TRAIN	21-9-17		Coy entrained about 1.15 am. departed BAILLEUL 2.18 am arriving BAPAUME. 12.15 pm On arrival Coy marched to BARASTRE and both our Commitment	Maj. B.

A6945 Wt. W11422/M1160 359,000 12/16 D.D. & L. Forms/C./2118/14.

WAR DIARY
or
INTELLIGENCE SUMMARY.
(Erase heading not required.)

Army Form C. 2118.

Place	Date	Hour	Summary of Events and Information	Remarks and references to Appendices
			Camp. Entraining & Detraining of mules, horses & transport wagons accomplished without a hitch	Officer B.
BARASTRE	22.9.17		Company training	Officer B.
"	23.9.17		Company training. 2nd Lts Blower & Bridgman accompanied O.C. & 2i/c to reconnoitre the line near HARGICOURT. 2nd Lt Blower remained at A.D. of 102nd Coy to further examine the position. Lt J.A.D. Bell received orders to proceed to O.K. & report to No. 5 F.T.C. Frantham	Officer B.
"	24.9.17		Company proceeded by march route to camp near HAUT ALLAINES. Whole Coy are accommodated together	
HAUT ALLAINES	25.9.17		Company proceeded by motor lorry to BERNES & were billeted there 2i/c proceeded to Coy H.Q. of 102nd Coy to arrange for relief. 16 O.R's sent forward to the Gun positions to remain till teams should arrive	Officer B.
"	26.9.17		Company relieved 102nd Coy in line. Relief complete by 10.30 p.m. No casualties. Any Chief relief. 16 positions taken over. Newport received orders to move to HAMELET, details near ROISEL.	Officer B.
LINE	27.9.17		Work carried out being positions & dug outs. A.Q. at TEMPLEUX	Officer B.

WAR DIARY
or
INTELLIGENCE SUMMARY.
(Erase heading not required.)

Army Form C. 2118.

Place	Date	Hour	Summary of Events and Information	Remarks and references to Appendices
Line	28.9.17		Enemy making shelter & employing Reserve Gartun. Took on the line to as H.Q. Continued. 2 O.R's joined the Coy as reinforcements from the Base. 2/Lt A.H. Douglas joined the Coy from the Base. 1 O.R. Admitted to Hospital.	Apps B.
Line	29.9.17		Nil. Firing from several portions. 1750 rounds fired. 1 O.R. admitted to hospital.	Apps B
Line	30.9.17		Nil. Firing answered 13,750 rounds fired. Infantry in line reported stampeding transport.	Apps B

C. P. Bennett, Capt.
Commanding 93rd Machine Gun Company.

Instructions regarding War Diaries and Intelligence Summaries are contained in F. S. Regs., Part II. and the Staff Manual respectively. Title pages will be prepared in manuscript.

WAR DIARY

or

~~INTELLIGENCE SUMMARY~~.

(Erase heading not required.)

Army Form C. 2118.

Place	Date	Hour	Summary of Events and Information	Remarks and references to Appendices
Confidential.			43rd. Machine Gun Company for the month of October 1917	Vol 19

2353 Wt. W2544/1454 700,000 5/15 D. D. & L. A.D.S.S. Forms/C. 2118.

Army Form C. 2118.

WAR DIARY
or
INTELLIGENCE SUMMARY.
(Erase heading not required.)

Instructions regarding War Diaries and Intelligence Summaries are contained in F.S. Regs., Part II. and the Staff Manual respectively. Title pages will be prepared in manuscript.

Place	Date	Hour	Summary of Events and Information	Remarks and references to Appendices
LWE	1-10-17		Improving & revetting trenches & emplacements. Indirect harassing fire on roads & tracks. 14000 rounds fired. 4 O.R. returned from leave to U.K.	Appx B.
"	2-10-17		Four guns withdrawn from line to ZOSAC at Coy. H.Q. leaving twelve positions in front. Support & Reserve lines. 8500 rounds fired from indirect fire positions. 2 O.R. admitted to F.A. (wounded)	Appx B.
"	3-10-17		Work carried on revetting & building up trenches. 10500 rounds fired at what are supposed targets. 1 O.R. admitted to F.A. 1 O.R. died of wounds. 2 O.R. evacuated to C.C.S.	Appx B.
"	4-10-17		Alternative emplacements commenced. 7500 rounds fired by indirect fire. 1 O.R. admitted to hospital. 2/Lt C.W. Hunt joined the Coy from the Base.	Appx B.
"	5-10-17		Alternative emplacements continued. 7500 rounds fired. 7500 rounds fired by harassing fire. 7 O.R. proceeded on leave to U.K.	Appx B.
"	6-10-17		Work on alternative positions carried on. 7500 rounds fired on indirect targets. 2/Lt Brown admitted to hosp. 1 O.R. admitted to hosp. 2 O.R. rejoined from leave.	Appx B.
"	7-10-17		Work of revetting trenches also in position carried on. Weather colder.	Appx B.

Army Form C. 2118.

WAR DIARY
or
INTELLIGENCE SUMMARY.
(Erase heading not required.)

Instructions regarding War Diaries and Intelligence Summaries are contained in F. S. Regs., Part II. and the Staff Manual respectively. Title pages will be prepared in manuscript.

Place	Date	Hour	Summary of Events and Information	Remarks and references to Appendices
LINE			So this went became any important	
	8-10-17		Relief & Distr of position accomplished as per attached operation order.	Apx 3
			8 O.R.s joined Coy from Infantry Base. Company attached	Apx 2
	9-10-17		Resisting Shipping Trenches 8500 rounds fired during night. 1 O.R. admitted	
			to Hospital. 1 O.R. Evacuated to I.C.S.	Apx 3
"	10-10-17		Resisting Trenches Entrained. 7750 rounds fired during night. Indirect fire	
			One O.R. admitted to Hospital	Apx 3
"	11-10-17		Resisting Trenches Entrained. 2250 rounds fired during night. Indirect fire	
			1 O.R. Evacuated to I.C.S. 2/Lt Rofen appointed Transport Officer	Apx 3
			vice Lt Bell (to U.K.)	Apx 3
"	12-10-17		Resisting Trenches. Check Shooting. 4250 rounds fired during night.	Apx 3
"	13-10-17		Resisting Trenches. 5000 rounds fired during night	Apx 3
	14-10-17		Resisting Trenches. 3000 rounds fired during the night.	
			Company Whistled itself in this line. No 3 under 2/Lt. Ongley's Canera	
			into Reserve.	Plc4

Army Form C. 2118.

WAR DIARY
or
INTELLIGENCE SUMMARY.
(Erase heading not required.)

Instructions regarding War Diaries and Intelligence Summaries are contained in F. S. Regs., Part II. and the Staff Manual respectively. Title pages will be prepared in manuscript.

Place	Date	Hour	Summary of Events and Information	Remarks and references to Appendices
TEMPLEUX	12/10/17		Lieut Bennet proceeded from 12th M.G. Company as an appointment as Commanding Officer of that unit and was struck off the strength of this unit accordingly	
	15/10/17		1 O.R. proceeded to III Corps School of instruction for 10 days a course.	Nil.
			2 O.Rs. discharged from Hospital	
			2 1 O.R. admitted to Hospital	
			1 O.R. evacuated to C.C.S.	
			Lt. Amphlett took over acting 2/in Command	Nil.
			1 O.R. admitted to Hospital.	
	16/10/17		Resting and unloading of trucks continued. 4000 rounds	
			were fired during the night.	
			1 O.R. admitted to Hospital	
			1 O.R. discharged from Hospital	Nil.
	17/10/17		Trucks cleared and written 5000 rounds fired during the night.	Nil.
			2 O.Rs. admitted to Hospital.	

Army Form C. 2118.

WAR DIARY
or
INTELLIGENCE SUMMARY.
(Erase heading not required.)

Instructions regarding War Diaries and Intelligence Summaries are contained in F. S. Regs., Part II. and the Staff Manual respectively. Title pages will be prepared in manuscript.

Place	Date	Hour	Summary of Events and Information	Remarks and references to Appendices
TEMPLEUX	18/10/17		Continued repair of trenches and improvement of emplacements.	
			3 O.Rs admitted to Hospital.	
			6 O.Rs proceeded on leave to U.K.	Plun.
	19/10/17		8000 rounds fired during the night.	
			1 O.R. wounded (accidentally)	
			1 O.R. admitted to Hospital.	Plun.
	20/10/17		4000 rounds of S.A.A. fired during the night.	
			1 O.R. returned from leave to U.K.	Plun.
	21/10/17		Relief and change of position as per attached table No 3.	
			No 4 Section under 2/Lt. HIRST in reserve.	
			3000 rounds fired during the night.	
			1 O.R. proceeded on leave to PARIS.	Plun.
	22/10/17		3500 rounds fired during the night. Burthing and draining of trenches continued.	Plun.
	23/10/17		4000 rounds fired during the night.	
			1 O.R. joined as reinforcement from the Base.	Plun.

WAR DIARY
INTELLIGENCE SUMMARY
(Erase heading not required.)

Army Form C. 2118.

Place	Date	Hour	Summary of Events and Information	Remarks and references to Appendices
TEMPLEUX	24/9/17		3100 rounds fired during the night to supplement repairs and finishes noted.	
			1 O.R. admitted to Hospital	
			1 O.R. evacuated to C.C.S.	OMM.
			1 O.R. transferred to III Corps Convalescent Camp.	
"	25/9/17		4000 rounds fired during the night. Continued work on trenches	OMM.
	26/9/17		Co-operated with Artillery in conjunction on the raid 7-2 W Brigade. 2 cal 700 rounds on Malakoff and RUBY WOOD	
			1 O.R. admitted to Hospital	OMM.
	27/9/17		Commenced building new dugout in GUSTAR ROAD.	
			1 O.R. evacuated to C.C.S.	
			5 O.R. joined the Company as reinforcement	OMM.
	28/9/17		4000 rounds fired during the night on enemy track and lines of communication.	
			2 /Lt. Duff was admitted to Hospital	OMM.

WAR DIARY
or
INTELLIGENCE SUMMARY.

Army Form C. 2118.

Place	Date	Hour	Summary of Events and Information	Remarks and references to Appendices
TEMPLEUX	28/4/17		Company Whist to Place as per attached table.	Nil.
"	29/4/17		Indirect firing carried out, 8500 rounds being fired.	
			1 O.R. proceeded on a course of Instruction at VII Corps Gas School. OR 5 returned from leave to UK	
"	30/4/17		Vickers Guns fired 3450 rounds on various targets during the night of the 29/30th	
"	31		Night firing resumed, 4250 rounds being fired. Notification received that 2/Lieut FINCH. G.F. has been granted a MEDICAL BOARD and is struck off the strength of this Unit.	

(signature) Captain
COMMANDING No 73 M.G. COY.
MACHINE GUN CORPS.

SECRET.   Copy No... 4 ......

                         73rd Machine Gun Company.

                            OPERATION ORDER BY

                         Captain. C.E.R. Croager. M.C.
                                    for
                    Relief and change over of Positions on the 14th inst.

                                                          13/10/17.

1. No.3.Section under 2/Lieut. DOUGLAS will come into Reserve.

2. No.1.Section under 2/Lt. BLAIR will take over Nos. 9, 10, 11, & 12
   positions from No.2.Section.

3. No.2. Section under 2/Lt. BRIDGEMAN will take over Nos. 1, 2, 3, & 4.
   positions from No.4.Section.
       i.e. Team at present at No.12 position will take over No.1. position.
            do.   No.11.   do.   do.   No.2.   do.
            do.   No.10.   do.   do.   No.3.   do.
            do.   No. 9.   do.   do.   No.4.   do.

4. No.4.Section under Lieut. WOOD will take over Nos. 5, 6, 13, & 14.
   positions from No.3.Section.
       i.e. Team at present at No.1.position will take over No.14 position.
            do.   No.2.   do.   do.   No.13. do.
            do.   No.3.   do.   do.   No.5.   do.
                         No.4.   do.   do.   No.6.   do.

5. 2/Lieut. BLAIR with No.1.Section will leave Coy. H.Q. at 11.a.m. When in
   in the line he will, in addition to his four teams, be in charge of one
   team of No.4. Section at No.13. position.

6. 2/Lieut. CRACKNELL, immediately on relief will bring No.2.Section to Coy.
   H.Q. whence they will be taken by 2/Lt. BRIDGEMAN to Nos.1, 2, 3, & 4.
   positions.

7. Lt. WOOD on arrival of 2/Lt.BRIDGEMAN, will send teams from Nos.1 & 2.
   positions to Coy. H.Q. whence they will be guided to Nos.13 & 14 positions
   He will then take teams from Nos.3 & 4 positions to 2/Lieut. Douglas'
   Section H.Q. 2/Lieut. Douglas will arrange for one team to be guided to
   No.5 position. 2/Lieut. Hirst will be in charge of Nos. 5 & 6 positions.

8. 2/Lieut. Douglas on relief will proceed with his two teams to Coy. H.Q.

9. Lieut. Wood will be in charge of the one team of No.4 section at No.14
   position.

10. Rations will be taken to all sections H.Q.

11. All Officers in the line will, when sending in their first morning report
    forward ~~send in~~ a list of each of their teams. This is essential to the correct
    distribution of rations.

12. List of trench stores etc. taken over must be forwarded to Coy. H.Q. as
    soon as possible after relief.

13. Officers are reminded that their morning reports must reach Coy. H.Q.
    by 8.30.a.m. each morning at the latest. *which must be accurately compiled*

14. All guns, trench stores, maps, etc., will be handed over.

15. All work in progress and proposed will be handed over, and a copy of this
    ~~will be~~ forwarded to Coy. H.Q. by the relieved Officer.

        Issued at 8.45.p.m.
            "   " 11.30pm   C.E.R.Croager
                                                    Captain,
                            Commanding 73rd Machine Gun Company.
    Copy No. 1. 73rd Inf.Bde. No.5. War Diary.   ~~No. 9.~~ 2/Lt. Blair.
             2. File.   No.6. Lt. Andrews. ~~No.10.~~ 2/Lt. Douglas.
             3. War diary.   No.7. Lt. Wood.   No.11. 2/Lt. Hirst.
             4. War diary.   No.8. 2/Lt. Bridgeman. ~~No.12.~~ ~~2/Lt. Cracknell.~~

SECRET
4.

O P E R A T I O N   O R D E R
-:by:-
Captain. C.E.M. Croager. M.C.
Commanding 73rd Machine Gun Company.
for
Relief and change over of positions on the 21st inst.

20/10/17.

(1.) No.4. Section under 2/Lt. HIRST will come in to Reserve at Coy. H.Q.

(2.) One team of No.2.Section and 3 teams of No.3.Section under 2/Lt. DOUGLAS. will take over S.4. F.3. F.4. & F.5. from Nos. 1. & 4. Sections.

(3.) 2 Teams of No.1.Section under Lt.WOOD will take over F.1. & S.1 from No.2. Section.

(4.) 2. Teams of No.1.Section and 1 team of No.2.Section will take over F.2. S.2. & S.3. under 2/Lt. CRACKNELL.

(5.)

(5.) 1 team of No.3.Section and 2 teams of No.2. take over R.3. R.2. & R.1., under 2/Lt. Bridgeman. i.e.

Teams at present at F.1. will take over R.2.
do.   F.2. will come into Reserve.
do.   F.3. will take over S.1.
do.   F.4. do.   do. F.1.
do.   F.5. do.   do. S.3.
do.   S.1. do.   do. R.1.
do.   S.2. do.   do. F.2.
do.   S.3. do.   do. S.4.
do.   S.4. will come into Reserve.
do.   R.1. will come into Reserve.
do.   R.2. will come into Reserve.
do.   R.3. will take over S.2.

(6.) No.3.Section will leave Coy.H.Q. at 10.0.a.m. and report to 2/Lt. DOUGLAS at ORCHARD POST. When in the line, he will, in addition to the 3 teams of No.3.Section, be in charge of 1 team of No.2.Section at S.4.

(7.) Lt.WOOD. will relieve 2/Lt. BRIDGEMAN at S.1.
2/Lt. BRIDGEMAN will relieve 2/Lt. CRACKNELL at R.1.
2/Lt. CRACKNELL will relieve 2/Lt. HIRST at F.2.

(8.) The teams from F.1. F.5. R.3. F.3. & F.4. will proceed to Coy.H.Q whence they will be guided to their new positions.

(9.) Officers will be in charge of teams as follows:-
Lt. WOOD. will be in charge of F.1. & S.1.
2/Lt. CRACKNELL   do.   S.2. S.3. & F.2.
2/Lt. DOUGLAS.   do.   F.5. F.3. F.4. & S.4.
2/Lt. BRIDGEMAN   do.   R.1. R.2. & R.3.

(10.) Rations will be taken to all Section Headquarters.

(11.) All Officers, in the line, will, when sending in their first morning report send in a list of each of their teams. This is essential for the correct distribution of rations.

(12.) Lists of Trench Stores, etc, taken over must be forwarded to Coy H.Q. as soon as possible after relief.

(13.) Officers are reminded that their morning reports must reach Coy. H.Q. by 8.30.a.m. each morning.

(14.) All guns, trench stores, maps, etc will be handed over.

(15.) All work in the line, in progress and proposed will be handed over and a copy of this forwarded to Coy. H.Q. by the relieved Officer.

Issued at 6.0.p.m.
20/10/17.

[signature]
Captain.,
Commanding 73rd Machine Gun Company.

Copies to.
No.1. 73rd Inf.Bde.   3.-5. War Diary. No.6. File.
7. -. 17. All Officers. 18. C.S.M. 19. C.Q.M.S.

SECRET.   Copy No.......
                            OPERATION ORDER NO.4.
                                   -:by:-
                         Captain. C.E.R. Croager M.C.
                       Commanding 73rd Machine Gun Company.
                                                                    26/10/17.

1.   The 164th M.G.Coy. will relieve this Company's positions at R.3. TOINE POST, S.4. HUSSAR POST, and F.5. LITTLE BENJAMIN POST during the afternoon of the 26th inst.

2.   The Officers concerned will arrange to send a guide from each of these teams to the Section H.Qtrs. of 164th M.G.Coy at F.15.d.9.7. (opposite last house on left side of BELLICOURT Rd facing East) They must report not later than 2.0.p.m. Upon relief, teams will march independently to Coy. H.Q. and report there.

3.   Officers concerned will arrange to have the most responsible gun number remain with the incoming teams until some time the following day. Limbers for for guns, belt boxes, etc, will be at ORCHARD POST at 4.30.p.m.

4.   The 72nd M.G.Coy. will relieve this Company's positions at F.1. RUBY LANE, F.2. RIFLE PIT TRENCH, S.1. POND TRENCH S.2.&.3. SUNKEN ROAD, R.1. HARGICOURT TRENCH on the night of the 26/27th and morning of the 27th inst.

5.   2/Lt. HIRST will arrange to have guides for F.2. S.2.&.S.3. at Cross Roads HARGICOURT L.5.c.20.35. by 4.30.p.m. on 26th inst. Teams will carry all guns etc. to R.1. position and dump them there, and then proceed to above mentioned place. (para.3.)

6.   2/Lt. BRIDGEMAN will arrange for a guide to be at L.1c.a.40.70. Battn. H.Q. at 2.0.a.m. on the 27th inst to guide in team to R.1.

7.   No guides will be required for F.1. and S.1. positions. Incoming teams will report during morning of the 27th.

8.   No.R.3. will not be relieved but will be withdrawn during afternoon of 26th, dumping all guns, etc., at ORCHARD POST and wait the arrival of the limber.

9.   Transport will be at R.1. at 2.30.p.m. 27th inst. to convey guns, etc. of Nos. F.1. S.1. S.2. S.3. F.2. and R.1. to Coy. H.Q. The N.C.O. at R.1. will find the necessary guard for this equipment.

10. All belt boxes and belts in position will be handed over to 72nd M.G. Coy as trench stores, but not in the case of teams being relieved by 164th M.G.Coy.

11. Lists of Trench stores, etc., handed over will be forwarded to Coy. H.Q. receipted as early as possible. Copies of work in hand, and work proposed handed over by Officers will be forwarded to Coy. H.Q.

12. Officers will arrange for a responsible man to remain with each relieving team until the following day.

13. Carrying party of 13 men will report to 2/Lt.DOUGLAS on morning of the 26th inst.

14. Great care must be taken by Officers and N.C.O's in handing over, which must be very thorough. Care must also be taken to hand over only trench stores and not articles belonging to this Company, with the exception of belt boxes which will be handed over to 72nd M.G.Coy.

15. Two teams of No.4.Section will relieve the two teams at present at BENJAMIN POST at 11.0.a.m. on the 26th inst.

    Issued at. 8.30.a.m.   Captain.,
    26/10/17.   Commanding 73rd Machine Gun Company.

    Cpy No.1. 73rd Inf.Bde.   No.6. War Diary.   No.13. Lt.Rogers.
         2. 72nd M.G.Coy.   No.7.   do.   14. " Douglas.
         3. 164th M.G.Coy.   No.8. C.O.   No.15. C.S.M.
         4. File.   No.9. Lt.Andrews.   No.16. C.Q.M.S.
         5. War Diary.   No.10. Lt. Wood.

SECRET.   Copy No. 12

OPERATION ORDER No.5.
by
Captain. C.E.R.Croager. M.C.
Commanding 73rd Machine Gun Company.

28/10/17.

1. No.2.Section will come into Reserve.

2. 2 Teams of No.3.Section, (At present in reserve,) will relieve F.1. &
   S.1., which will relieve R.1. & F.2. respectively. R.1. & F.2. will
   then proceed to Coy. H.Q.

3. No.3.Section will march off from Coy. H.Q. at 11.0.a.m.

4. 2/Lt. BRIDGEMAN will return to Coy. H.Q. and will be in charge of teams
   at R.1. & R.2.

5. Lt.WOOD, 2/Lt.DOUGLAS. and 2/Lt. HIRST will remain in, and be in
   charge of their present positions.

6. All guns, equipment, trench stores, etc., will be handed over in the
   usual way. A list of trench stores will be forwarded to the CSM by
   6.0.p.m. on the 28th inst by all teams.

7. Work in progress and proposed will be handed over by N.C.O's i/c of
   relieved teams, and carried on with by the remaining teams. Reports
   on same will be forwarded by officers to Coy. H.Q. on the day
   following the relief.

8. Rations will be delivered at all Section Headquarters.

9. Handing over must be thoroughly done by N.C.O's of relieved teams.

            Issued at 8.0.a.m.
            28/10/17.   Sgd. C.E.R.Croager. Captain.,
                            Commanding 73rd Machine Gun Company.

                    Copy No.1. 73rd Inf. Bde.
                         2. Commanding officer.
                         3. Lieut. P.H.Andrews.
                         4. File.
                         5. 2/Lt. Bridgeman.
                         6. Lieut. Wood.
                         7. 2/Lt. Hirst.
                         8. 2/Lt. Douglas.
                         9. C.SM.
                        10. C.Q.M.Sgt.
                        11. War diary.
                        12.   do.
                        13.   do.

Army Form C. 2118.

WAR DIARY
or
INTELLIGENCE SUMMARY.
(Erase heading not required.)

Vol 20

73rd Machine Gun Company

for the Month of

November 1917

Place	Date	Hour	Summary of Events and Information	Remarks and references to Appendices

WAR DIARY
or
INTELLIGENCE SUMMARY.
(Erase heading not required.)

Army Form C. 2118.

Place	Date	Hour	Summary of Events and Information	Remarks and references to Appendices
TEMPLEUX-le-GUERARD	Nov. 1st		O.R. 1 returned from leave to PARIS. O.R.S 4 granted leave to the U.K.	
			O.R.s 3 found as reinforcements from the M.G.C. Base Depot. Firing the night of 31/1st 6500 rounds were fired on various targets.	MM
	2nd		O.R. 1 evacuated to hospital O.R.s discharged from hospital O.R.s granted leave to U.K. 9500 rounds were fired at usual night firing targets during the night of the 1st/2nd.	MM
	3rd		Further shoot carried out as per operation order Not attached. Indirect Firing carried out 6500 rounds being fired.	MM
	4th		2/LIEUT G. GOURLAY reported from base to U.K. night firing carried out on usual targets, Tatins near Quennemont Farm and BELLICOURT Road were swept during the night by out guns, 9500 Rounds being fired.	MM
	5th		A snipelist enemy machine gun enfilement was engaged and silenced after 250 rounds. In all 9500 rounds were fired on tracks and enemy back areas.	MM

WAR DIARY
or
INTELLIGENCE SUMMARY.
(Erase heading not required.)

Army Form C. 2118.

Place	Date	Hour	Summary of Events and Information	Remarks and references to Appendices
TEMPLEUX le GUERARD	Nov 6th		2/LIEUT G.W. HIRST and ORs 2 proceeded on a course of Instruction at G.H.Q Small Arms School. ORs 1 evacuated to CCS	
	7th		6500 rounds were fired at usual targets during the night	
			OR₂ admitted to hospital	
	8th		6000 rounds were fired at usual targets during the night	
			1/2 admitted to hospital	
	9th		6000 rounds were fired as usual. Carpet during the night. 10R arrived at No 11 hospital	
	9th		5 OR granted leave to U.K.	
	10th		9710 rounds fired during the night. Company roll off took place in the time during the day, and w.ft. & 2R per attend talks	
			10R discharged from Hosp T.U	
	11th		6000 rounds fired during the night	
	12th		3 ORs evacuated to CCS	
			1 OR discharged from CCS	
			9000 rounds fired during the night	

Army Form C. 2118.

WAR DIARY
or
INTELLIGENCE SUMMARY.
(Erase heading not required.)

Instructions regarding War Diaries and Intelligence Summaries are contained in F. S. Regs., Part II. and the Staff Manual respectively. Title pages will be prepared in manuscript.

Place	Date	Hour	Summary of Events and Information	Remarks and references to Appendices
TEMPLEUX	12/4/17		1 O.R. rejoined the Company from D.R.S.	
			O.Rs. proceeded on leave to U.K.	P.M.R.
		12.30	trench fires during the night.	
	13/4/17		1 O.R. discharged from 41. C.C.S. and rejoined company.	M.R.
		10.00	trench wiring fired during the night.	
		3.000	trench " " " " "	
	14/4/17		2/Lt. Conway G.K. slightly wounded in action	
			1 O.R. wounded in action (remaining at duty)	M.R.
	15/4/17		1 O.R. admitted to hospital.	
			6 O.Rs. proceeded on leave to U.K.	
			Capt. E.S.R. Brozer M.C. proceeded on leave to U.K.	M.R.
	16/4/17		9750 trench wire fired in conjunction with raid by 7th Northumb.	
	17/4/17		2 O.Rs. evacuated to C.C.S.	
			1 attached O.R. admitted to hospital.	
	18/4/17		3750 trench fires during the night.	P.M.R.
			1 O.R. admitted to hospital.	

WAR DIARY or INTELLIGENCE SUMMARY

Army Form C. 2118.

Place	Date	Hour	Summary of Events and Information	Remarks and references to Appendices
TEMPLEUX	18/4/17		1 O.R. admitted, discharged from Hospital.	nil
ATHIES-COURT	19/4/17		2 O.R. admitted to Hospital. Coy. H.Q. moved to ATHIES COURT.	nil
			Damage experienced whilst closing the night, and extra fuss and control put into position. at 6.50 p.m. cooperated with the raid by the 2/6th Leinsters. — the 6/4 P.W.T. Word. 1 O.R. evacuated to C.C.S. 1 attached O.R. " "	
	20/4/17		1 O.R. proceeded R.A.R. to take up communication. Coy H.Q. moved back to TEMPLEUX.	nil
TEMPLEUX	21/4/17		5 O.Rs. proceeded on leave to U.K. returned from leave.	nil
	22/4/17		1 O.R. evacuated to C.C.S. 2 " attd. " " to Hospital. 13000 rounds were fired during the night. Every M.G. opened	nil

WAR DIARY
or
INTELLIGENCE SUMMARY

Army Form C. 2118.

Place	Date	Hour	Summary of Events and Information	Remarks and references to Appendices
TEMPLEUX	23/11/17		Nil	Nil
	24/11/17		1 O.R. rejoined the Company, rest, recent from PERONNE. Capt. T.O. RAWTHORPE joins the Company as C.O. 10 R2O recruits find and during the night.	PLM
	25/11/17		2/Lt. CARLISLE BARNET joins the Company as reinforcement. Capt. CBR. CRO POSR. M.C. posted to M.G.T.C. GRANTHAM. 24th Div. A 92/89. dated 20/11/17. 6 O.Rs. proceeded on leave to U.K.	PLM
	26/11/17		2 O.Rs. discharged from Hospital. 1 O.R. evacuated to C.C.S. 6 O.Rs. proceeded on leave to U.K. 3 O.Rs. returned from leave.	PLM
	27/11/17		Nil	PLM
	28/11/17		1 O.R. wounded in action. 2/Lt. M.S INTYRE. W.M. joined the Company a reinforcement from HOLMES. H.C. " " " " PICKER Lt. T " " " "	PLM

WAR DIARY
or
INTELLIGENCE SUMMARY.
(Erase heading not required.)

Army Form C. 2118.

Place	Date	Hour	Summary of Events and Information	Remarks and references to Appendices
TEMPLEUX	29/6/17		2/Lt. H.C.T.B. moved the Company & returned from the Base. 4 O.Rs. returned from leave.	Pass
"	30/6/17		Being attached to the 11th Division. 4 guns attached to this Company from 72nd Company, and 1 Section from 191. Company. 3 guns of this Company were sent to reinforce 15th Div. at midday. TEMPLEUX heavily shelled all day. 4 O.Rs. wounded in action. 1 O.R. returned from Course of instruction. 1 O.R. proceeded to Course of instruction.	Ans
"	1/7/17			

M. Amherst Ln for
Lt. 73rd M.G. Coy.

Secret.   Copy No. 2

OPERATION ORDER, No.7.
-:by:-
Captain. C.E.R.Croager. M.C.
Commanding 73rd Machine Gun Company.

8/11/17.

1.   The following reliefs will take place during the day and night of the 9th inst.

2.   No.1.Section, which is now in reserve, will proceed to the line and No.3.Section into Company Reserve.

3.   The teams of No.1.Section will relieve F.3., F.4. & F.5.
F.5.Team will relieve S.2. who relieve S.1. who return to Coy. H.Q.
F.4.   do.   F.2.   do.   R.2.   do.
F.3.   do.   S.3.   do.   S.4.   do.
        1 team of No.1.Section will relieve R.3. who return to billets.
        Team at R.1. will relieve F.1. who will relieve R.1.

4.   The four teams of No.1.Section will march off to their respective positions from Coy. H.Q. at 9.0.a.m. R.1. team will relieve F.1. team by 11.0.a.m. N.C.O's will arrange to have a responsible Machine gunner to hand over to incoming team. He will then rejoin his team at F.1. position.

5.   2/Lieut. GOURLAY will relieve 2/Lieut. BRIDGEMAN in RIFLE PIT Tr. who will then relieve Lieut. ANDREWS, who will then return to Coy.H.Q.
        Separate instructions will be given to Lt. WOOD.

6.   After relief, 2/Lt. BRIDGEMAN will be in command of the following teams:- R.3., F.5., F.4., F.3., & S.4., and 2/Lt.GOURLAY in command of F.1., F.2., S.1., S.2., & S.3., Lt. WOOD will remain as at present.

7.   Rations, material, etc., as before.

8.   N.C.O's in charge must make absolutely certain that their dugout, emplacement and trench is absolutely clean before handing over. N.C.O's will not take over until the above are satisfactory.

9.   All Officers in the line, will, when sending in their first morning report, forward a list of each of their teams. This is essential for the correct distribution of rations.

10.   Lists of trench stores, etc., taken over must be forwarded to Coy. H.Q. as soon as possible after relief.

11.   Officers are reminded that their morning reports must reach Coy H.Q. by 8.30.a.m. at the latest, and must be accurately compiled.

12.   All guns, Trench stores, etc. will be handed over.

13.   All work in progress and proposed will be handed over and a copy of this will be forwarded to Coy. H.Q. by the relieved Officer.

        Issued at 11.45.p.m.   [signature]
        8/11/17.   Captain,
                            Commanding 73rd Machine Gun Company.

        Copy No. 1. 73rd Inf. Bde.   5. War Diary.   9. Lt. Wood.
                 2. C. O.   6.   - do -   10. 2/Lt.Rogers.
                 3. File.   7. Lt.Andrews.11. " Bridgeman.
                 4. War Diary.   8. 2/Lt.Gourlay.12. C.S.M.

S E C R E T.   Copy No. 3

           O P E R A T I O   O R D E R No. 8.
                        -:by:-
                 Lieutenant. P.M.Andrews.
            Commanding 73rd Machine Gun Company.
                                                    14/11/17.

1.   The following reliefs will take place in the line on the 15th and night of the 15th/16th.

2.   No.4. Section will come into reserve at Coy. H.Q.

3.   4 teams of No.3. Section will relieve F.3., F.4., F.5., And R.3., respectively.

        relief F.3. will relieve S.3. who relieve S.4. who come into reserve.
        do.   F.4.   do.   S.2.   do.   R.2.   do.
        do.   F.5.   do.   F.2.   do.   F.1. WHO relieve R.1. do. do.
        do.   R.3.   do.   S.1. who come into reserve.

4.   No.3. Section will march off from Coy. H.Q. at 8.30 a.m. under Cpl. BATHURST.

5.   Lieut. WOOD will ~~relieve 2/Lieut. GOURLAY~~ proceed to F.2. position. ~~2/Lieut. GOURLAY will relieve 2/Lieut. BRIDGEMAN at R.3.~~ Remain at R.3.

6.   ~~2/Lieut. BRIDGEMAN will come to Coy. H.Q. after relief.~~
        Lieut. WOOD will be i/c of F.1., S.1., F.2., S.2., S.3.,
        ~~2/Lieut.GOURLAY do.   do.   F.4., F.4., F.5., R.4., R.5.,~~
        2/Lieut. BRIDGEMAN do.   ~~R.1., R.1.~~ F3, F4, F5, S4, R3

7.   Rations will be at HARGICOURT DUMP at 7.0 p.m.
            do.   do.   ORCHARD POST   at 7.0 p.m.
            do. for R.2., and R.3., will be taken off at ORCHARD POST.
        The limber will then proceed to HUSSAR ROAD, whence rations for S.4., F.5., and F.3., will be taken off. The Officer i/c left group will provide a guide. The limber will be at HUSSAR ROAD at 7.30 p.m. This dump will in future be known as HUSSAR DUMP.

8.   Handing over of positions to be thorough. All emplacements, dugouts latrines etc, to be left clean.

9.   Lists of trench stores taken over, to be sent in to Coy H.Q. on the first morning report after relief.

10.   All guns equipment and trench stores to be handed over.

11.   All work in hand and proposed, to be thoroughly handed over.

            Issued at 5.0 p.m.
            14/11/17.
                                                        Lieutenant,
                                            Commanding 73rd Machine Gun Company.

        Copy No. 1. 73rd Inf. Bde.   5. War Diary.   9. 2/Lt. Bridgeman.
                2. C.O.   6.   -do-   10. Rogers.
                3. File.   7. Lt. Wood.   11. C.S.M.
                4. War Diary.   ~~8. 2/Lt. Gourlay.~~

SECRET.   Copy No. 4

OPERATION ORDER. No 9.
-:by:-
Lieutenant. P. H. Andrews.
Commanding 73rd Machine Gun Company.

21/11/17.

1. The following reliefs will take place in the line on the 22nd and night of the 22/23rd.

2. No. 2. Section will come into reserve at Coy. H.Q.

3. 4 teams of No. 4. Section will relieve F.3., F.4., F.5., and R.3., respectively.

On relief F.5. will relieve S.3. who relieve R.2. who come into reserve.
    do.   F.4.   do.   F.2.   do.   S.1.   do.
    do.   F.3.   do.   S.2.   do.   S.4.   do.
    do.   R.3.   come into reserve.

4. No. 4. Section will march off from Coy. H.Q. at 2.30 p.m. under Sgt. Evans.

5. Officers to remain as at present.

6. Rations for 2 days will be sent up as usual.

7. Handing over of positions to be thorough. All emplacements, dug-outs, latrines etc. to be left clean.

8. Lists of trench stores taken over, to be sent in to Coy. H.Q. on the first morning after relief.

9. All gun equipment and trench stores to be handed over.

10. All work in hand and proposed, to be thoroughly handed over.

11. Particular attention to be paid to handing over instructions for harrassing fire.

    Issued at 10.0 p.m.   P. H. Andrews   Lieut.
    21/11/17.   Commanding 73rd Machine Gun Company.

Copy. No. 1. 73rd Inf. Bde.   No. 5 War Diary.   No. 9. 2/Lt. Rogers.
         2. C.O.   6. do.   11. C.S.M.
         3. File.   7. Lt. Wood.
         4. War Diary.   8. 2/Lt. Bridgeman.

SECRET.   Copy. No.....

OPERATION ORDER. No. 10.
-:by:-
Captain. J.B.Gawthorpe.
Commanding 73rd Machine Gun Company.
27/11/17.

1. The following reliefs will take place in the line on the 28th inst. and night of the 28/29th inst.

2. No. 1. Section will come into reserve, at Coy. H.Q.

3. 4 teams of No. 2. Section will relieve F.3., F.4., F.5., and R.3. respectively.

On relief F.5. will relieve S.3. who relieve S.1. who come into reserve.
    do. F.4.   do.   S.4. who come into reserve.
    do. F.3.   do.   S.2. who relieve R.1. who come into reserve.
    do. R.3.   do.   F.1. do. R.2. do.
    F.2. will remain as at present.

4. No.2 Section will march off from Coy. H.Q. at 2.30 p.m. under Sgt. Reilly.

5. Officers to remain as at present.

6. Rations for 2 days will be sent up as usual.

7. Handing over of positions to be thorough. All emplacements, dugouts, latrines etc. to be left clean.

8. Lists of trench stores taken over, to be sent in to Coy.H.Q. on the first morning after relief.

9. All gun equipment and trench stores to be handed over.

10. All work in hand and proposed, to be thoroughly handed over.

11. Particular attention to be paid to handing over instructions for harrassing fire.

12. Trench reports to be sent to Coy. H.Q. by 8.20 a.m. at the latest.

Issued at 5.0 p.m.   Lieut.For Captain.
27/11/17.   Commanding 73rd Machine Gun Company.

Copy.No. 1. 73rd Inf. Bde.   No. 5. War Diary.   No.9. 2/Lt.Rogers.
        2. C.O.   6.   do.   10. 2/Lt.H.Carlis
        3. File.   7. Lt. Wood.   Bmlet
        4. War Diary.   8. 2/Lt. Bridgeman. 11. C.S.M.

Army Form C. 2118.

WAR DIARY
INTELLIGENCE SUMMARY.
(Erase heading not required.)

Place	Date	Hour	Summary of Events and Information	Remarks and references to Appendices

10th Australian Machine Gun Company

For the month of December 1917

Army Form C. 2118.

WAR DIARY
or
INTELLIGENCE SUMMARY.
(Erase heading not required.)

Instructions regarding War Diaries and Intelligence Summaries are contained in F. S. Regs., Part II. and the Staff Manual respectively. Title pages will be prepared in manuscript.

Place	Date	Hour	Summary of Events and Information	Remarks and references to Appendices
TEMPLEUX.	1/12/17		2 O.Rs. discharged from Hospital.	
	2/12/17		1 " proceeded to a course of Veterinary work. 3 gunners attached to 19th Div. rejoined the Company.	nil.
	3/12/17		1 O.R. returned from course of instruction at VII Corps School. 1 O.R. rejoined the Company from Hospital.	nil.
	4/12/17		Inter Company Rifle & Lewis Gun Competition. Capt. no 11. (Attached) 1 O.R. admitted to Hospital.	nil.
	5/12/17		2/Lt. HOLMES " " "	nil.
	6/12/17		1 O.R. proceeded to VII Corps School. 2/Lt (with Bty) raided enemy trenches. Mtrs. cooperated in the barrage. O.K.	nil.
	7/12/17		LIEUT. WOOD proceeded on leave to U.K. " " " " " B.O.TC.	nil.
	8/12/17		Usual harassing fire carried out nightly.	
	9/12/17		1 O.R. granted leave to U.K.	nil.

Army Form C. 2118.

WAR DIARY
or
INTELLIGENCE SUMMARY.
(Erase heading not required.)

Instructions regarding War Diaries and Intelligence Summaries are contained in F. S. Regs., Part II. and the Staff Manual respectively. Title pages will be prepared in manuscript.

Place	Date	Hour	Summary of Events and Information	Remarks and references to Appendices
TEMPLEUX	10/12/17		2 O.Rs. returned from leave. 1 O.R. proceeded to report to O.C. Reinforcements ETAPLES for release on mains I.D. WO authority.	PWR.
	11/12/17		D.A.G. A.H. 789 dated 7/12/17. 4 O.Rs. returned from leave to U.K. 9 O.R. Sinecure racibil enemy trenches. M.G's cooperated with Lewis G.F.	PWR.
	12/12/17		1 O.R. admitted to Hospital.	PWR.
	13/12/17		1 O.R. wounded accidentally.	
	14/12/17		1 O.R. returned from Corps of Instruction.	
	15/12/17		2 O.Rs. proceeded to U.K. for admission to Chest Units.	PWR.
	16/12/17		1 O.R. admitted to Hospital	PWR.
	17/12/17		4 O.Rs. rejoined the Company from the Base. 1 O.R. granted leave to U.K. 2/Lt. HOLMES rejoined the Company from Hospital	PWR.

WAR DIARY
INTELLIGENCE SUMMARY.
(Erase heading not required.)

Army Form C. 2118.

Place	Date	Hour	Summary of Events and Information	Remarks and references to Appendices
TEMPLEUX.	18/12/17		Company relieved in the line by the 17th M.G. Coy according to attached table. On relief this company proceeded to DETAIL CAMP HERVILLY. TEMPLEUX heavily shelled with 5.9.s during the morning, thus delaying the relief.	A/R.
HERVILLY	19/12/17		Company training commenced.	A5
	20/12/17		Training carried out. Rendered keen to inclement weather.	A5
	21/12/17		Training continued.	A5
	22/12/17		Training continued. 1 O.R. to U.K. leave. 1 O.R. to Hospital. Extract from LONDON GAZETTE 5/12/17. Regular forces. West Yorkshire Regt. Capt.(A/Major) J.B. Gawthorpe from T.F.(May 4.) to be Captains and to retain his higher rank on seniority whilst holding present appointment.	A5

WAR DIARY
~~INTELLIGENCE SUMMARY~~
(Erase heading not required.)

Army Form C. 2118.

Place	Date	Hour	Summary of Events and Information	Remarks and references to Appendices
HERVILLY	23/12/17		Infantry training. 2 O.R.s evacuated I.O.R. to hospital.	aa
	24/12/17		Extract from LONDON GAZETTE 24/12/17. 2/Lt. A.L. BLOWER Mentioned in Despatches for services in the field. 1 O.R. admitted to hospital.	aa
	25/12/17		2 O.R. evacuated C.C.S. Celebrated Xmas. Men were given an excellent dinner & tea ran. A cinema was given in the evening by 73rd M.G. Coy. 75th Bgde Trench Mortar Battery & 1 Middlesex Regt.	aa
	26/12/17		Went Holmes with No. 234 sections proceeded to TEMPLEUX to relieve 4 guns of 10th Cavalry M.G. Squadron and 4 guns of the 17th M.G. Coy in reserve.	aa

Army Form C. 2118.

WAR DIARY
or
INTELLIGENCE SUMMARY.
(Erase heading not required.)

Instructions regarding War Diaries and Intelligence Summaries are contained in F. S. Regs., Part II. and the Staff Manual respectively. Title pages will be prepared in manuscript.

Place	Date	Hour	Summary of Events and Information	Remarks and references to Appendices
TEMPLEUX	28/7/19		The 7th M.G. Coy. proceeded to relieve the 11th M.G. Coy. in the line as per the attached table.	aa
	29/7/19	10 A.M.	attached to Brigade.	aa
	29/7/19		M. Guns fired 1000 rounds on tracks.	aa
	30/7/19		Sent by rail	aa
	31/7/19		1 O.R. to hospital. 2/Lt BRIDGEMAN took over duties of Intelligence Officer	aa

(A7292). Wt. W12859/M1293. 750,000. 1/17. D. D. & L., Ltd. Forms/C.2118/14.

Army Form C. 2118.

WAR DIARY
INTELLIGENCE SUMMARY.
(Erase heading not required.)

Vol 22

Place	Date	Hour	Summary of Events and Information	Remarks and references to Appendices
Regimental			3rd machine gun company for the month of January 1918	

WAR DIARY
INTELLIGENCE SUMMARY

Army Form C. 2118.

Place	Date	Hour	Summary of Events and Information	Remarks and references to Appendices
TEMPLEUX	1/1/18		Capt. J.B. Gawthorpe proceeded to Div. H.Q. to take up duties of A/D.M.G.O.	AG
			I.O.R. proceeded to U.K. leave.	
			LIEUT. P.M. ANDREWS assumed command of the coy. "A" WOOD took over duties of 2nd in command.	
			Enemy machine gun in Quennet Copse silenced by fire of two of our guns.	SGB
TEMPLEUX	2/1/18		I.O.R. proceeded to U.K. for "Special" leave.	1/92
	3/1/18		9/L Douglas discharged from hospital	SGB
	4/1/18		75th M.G. Coy. relieved in the line by the 72 M.G. Coy. I.O.R. reported to 75th M.G. Coy.	SGB
HERVILLY	5/1/18		2nd Lt. Douglas reported to 75th M.G. Coy.	SGB

WAR DIARY
INTELLIGENCE SUMMARY
(Erase heading not required.)

Army Form C. 2118.

Place	Date	Hour	Summary of Events and Information	Remarks and references to Appendices
HERMILLY	5/1/18		1.O.R. rejoined the 73rd M.S. Coy.	1093
	6/1/18		2.O.Rs rejoined the 73rd M.S. Coy.	SE3
	7/1/18		4.O.Rs proceeded on leave to U.K.	SE3
			2.O.Rs proceeded for a Cruise to G.H.Q. S.A.S.	
			Lt. Andrews proceeded for Senior Officers Course to G.H.Q. 2nd A.	SE3
			73rd M.S. Coy. relieved in Div. Support by 17th M.S. Coy.	
			& proceeded to VRAIGNES for Div. Reserve.	
VRAIGNES	8/1/18		Training as per programme commenced as entire Coy.	SE3
			Coy. paraded for written practice on	
			Range at HANCOURT.	
	9/1/18		2.O.Rs admitted to hospital.	SE3
			1.O.R. rejoined from leave to U.K.	

Army Form C. 2118.

WAR DIARY
or
INTELLIGENCE SUMMARY.
(Erase heading not required.)

Instructions regarding War Diaries and Intelligence Summaries are contained in F. S. Regs., Part II. and the Staff Manual respectively. Title pages will be prepared in manuscript.

Place	Date	Hour	Summary of Events and Information	Remarks and references to Appendices
VRAIGNES	9/1/18		3 O.R.s appointed L/Cpls.	S.E.B
	10/1/18		Training as per programme but presented owing to inclement weather. Indoor training of Section on the gun, lectures to N.C.O.s then by Section Officers.	S.E.B
	11/1/18		Brigade practice operation cancelled owing to inclement weather. Special training for N.C.O.s of two 78th M.G. Cos on Map reading & the pneumatic compass by 2nd Lt Dryden.	S.E.B
	13/1/18		Afternoon devoted to sports. SUNDAY	S.E.B

WAR DIARY
or
INTELLIGENCE SUMMARY

Army Form C. 2118.

Instructions regarding War Diaries and Intelligence Summaries are contained in F.S. Regs., Part II. and the Staff Manual respectively. Title pages will be prepared in manuscript.

(Erase heading not required.)

Place	Date	Hour	Summary of Events and Information	Remarks and references to Appendices
VRAIGNES	12/1/18		1 O.R. admitted to Field Ambulance.	AB
	13/1/18		1 O.R. to Base & struck off strength accordingly. A highly successful smoking concert held in the mess hut.	e893
	14/1/18		Lt Cord, 2/Lts Brunlett, Holmes & Douglas attended a lecture at DALY'S THEATRE	SP
	15/1/18		Drawing. Special attention to training of N.C.Os. 2 O.R.s to U.K. leave.	Pas
	16/1/18		Officers & N.C.Os attended gas lecture by Div. gas officer at HANCOURT	Pas

WAR DIARY
or
INTELLIGENCE SUMMARY.

(Erase heading not required.)

Army Form C. 2118.

Place	Date	Hour	Summary of Events and Information	Remarks and references to Appendices
VRAIGNES	17/1/18		2/Lt Dicker, Macintyre & Stell attended a lecture on "Intelligence". Returned much benefit.	A5
	18/1/18		Company played "C" Coy 2nd Fenwick Regt. Result. M.G.C 4 goals 2 Fenwick Regt 0 goals.	A5
	19/1/18		Preparing for line. 1 O.R. admitted to hospital 1 O.R. reported from leave to U.K.	A5
HARGICOURT	20/1/18		123rd M.G. Coy relieved 11/Lth M.G. Coy in the line. Coy. HQ moved further forward from TEMPLEUX to HAGICOURT.	A5
	21/1/18		No 7 gun position acted and gun returned to position.	A5

WAR DIARY
INTELLIGENCE SUMMARY.

Army Form C. 2118.

Place	Date	Hour	Summary of Events and Information	Remarks and references to Appendices
HARGICOURT	26/1/18		Capt. J.B. Gaustope rejoined Coy. 1 O.R. proceeded to U.K. for a Cadet batt. 2 U.K's to GRANTHAM, for promotion course.	
	27/1/18		Enemy machine gun silenced by our fire. 2 Rfts. to U.K. leave 1 O.R. rejoined. 10 O.R's to base.	
	28/1/18		Enemy very quiet. Interior sustained fire by two of our guns caused an enemy M.G. firing from RUBY WOOD to cease fire.	
	29/1/18		Left Seaton H.Q. moved to HUSSAR RD. [illegible] in rear of N.P.	

WAR DIARY
or
INTELLIGENCE SUMMARY

Army Form C. 2118.

(Erase heading not required.)

Place	Date	Hour	Summary of Events and Information	Remarks and references to Appendices
HARGICOURT	26/1/18		An enemy M.G. opening from direction of Quennet Copse was silenced by our fire.	
	27/1/18		Defence scheme was revised. Enemy aeroplanes were driven off by fire from M.G. guns.	
	28/1/18		Sgt Rogers rejoined from C.C.S. 1 O.R. admitted to hospital	
HERVILLY	29/1/18		23rd M.G. Coy was relieved in line by 22nd M.G. Coy & proceeded to HERVILLY becoming Coy in outpost. 1 O.R. to hospital	
	30/1/18		Lt Maguire proceeded on leave to U.K. 2 O.Rs to hospital.	

WAR DIARY
INTELLIGENCE SUMMARY

Army Form C. 2118.

Place	Date	Hour	Summary of Events and Information	Remarks and references to Appendices
HERVILLY	3/11/18		"O.R." found no reinforcement from Base. Sgt McKAY granted Begium Croix de Guerre for services before Sept- 1917. Company retorned Cato.	

J Davis Lieut.
for OC 273rd Machine Gun Coy.

Army Form C. 2118.

Vol 23

WAR DIARY
~~INTELLIGENCE SUMMARY.~~
(Erase heading not required.)

Instructions regarding War Diaries and Intelligence Summaries are contained in F. S. Regs., Pars. II. and the Staff Manual respectively. Title pages will be prepared in manuscript.

Place	Date	Hour	Summary of Events and Information	Remarks and references to Appendices
~~Contents~~			1/2nd Machine Gun Company for the month of February 1918	

Army Form C. 2118.

WAR DIARY
or
INTELLIGENCE SUMMARY.

(Erase heading not required.)

Instructions regarding War Diaries and Intelligence Summaries are contained in F. S. Regs., Part II. and the Staff Manual respectively. Title pages will be prepared in manuscript.

Place	Date	Hour	Summary of Events and Information	Remarks and references to Appendices
HERVILLY	1/2/18		1 O.R. admitted to F.A.	MCB
HERVILLY	2/2/18		2 guns of 73rd M.G.Coy relieved 2 guns of 191 Coy on A.A. duty at ROISEL. 2 guns of 73rd M.G.Coy relieved 2 guns of 17th M.G.Coy on AA duty at HANCOURT. 2 guns of 73 M.G. Coy occupied a position at TOMBLEUX FARM.	MCB
HERVILLY	3/2/18		Sergt MURPHY. P. awarded Croix de Guerre. (Belgian). (31.1.18) 1 O.R. proceeded to 73rd Field Ambulance for a course of Rhapsody.	MCB

Army Form C. 2118.

WAR DIARY
or
INTELLIGENCE SUMMARY.
(Erase heading not required.)

Instructions regarding War Diaries and Intelligence Summaries are contained in F. S. Regs., Part II. and the Staff Manual respectively. Title pages will be prepared in manuscript.

Place	Date	Hour	Summary of Events and Information.	Remarks and references to Appendices
HERVILLY	4/3/18		1 O.R. proceeded to U.K. for commission. 10 O.Rs. evacuated to B.C.C.S.	MCB
HERVILLY	5/3/18		4 O.Rs. proceeded on leave to U.K.	MCB
			9 O.Rs. reinforcements	MCB
HERVILLY	6/3/18		5 O.Rs. reinforcements	MCB
HERVILLY	7/3/18		2 Officers and 6,400 reconnoitred the proposed positions in front of TEMPLEUX QUARRY.	MCB
HERVILLY	8/3/18		1 O.R. admitted to F.A.	MCB
HERVILLY	9/3/18		Corp. GAWTHORPE and 2LT. ARCHDALE - BARNET proceeded to B.R.I.N., T.D.S.A., BELLINCOURT Theatre of TANKS.	MCB

WAR DIARY or INTELLIGENCE SUMMARY

Army Form C. 2118.

Instructions regarding War Diaries and Intelligence Summaries are contained in F. S. Regs., Part II. and the Staff Manual respectively. Title pages will be prepared in manuscript.

(Erase heading not required.)

Place	Date	Hour	Summary of Events and Information	Remarks and references to Appendices
HELMIEH	10/9/18		2 Lt HR. CARLISLE-BAYLISS and servant admitted to E.A. 2 Lt HOLT and servant proceed to Ct Port and on P.T. course. 3 O.Rs rejoined from leave.	MCB
HELMIEH	11/9/18		I.O.R. evacuated to C.C.S. 1 O.R. rejoined from E.A.	MCB
HELMIEH	11/9/18		Lt ANDREWS and 2Lt ROGERS proceed to U.K. 2 O.R's to U.K for leave.	MCB
HELMIEH	12/9/18		Sgt. Clevers proceed for a typers course.	MCB

Army Form C. 2118.

WAR DIARY
or
INTELLIGENCE SUMMARY.
(Erase heading not required.)

Instructions regarding War Diaries and Intelligence
Summaries are contained in F. S. Regs., Part II.
and the Staff Manual respectively. Title pages
will be prepared in manuscript.

Place	Date	Hour	Summary of Events and Information	Remarks and references to Appendices
HERMIES	13/1/18		3 ORs. to U.K. on leave.	
			2 LT. RENNISON (BATTLETONE servant) rejoined from 7 A.	
			73 rd M.G. Coy. relieved the 7th M.G. Coy. in the line.	Map
MOEUVRES	14/4/18		10 R. evacuated to 6 C.C.S.	
			6 ORs. proceeded to U.K. for leave	MOB
HERMIES	14/4/18		2 OR rejoined from U.K.	MOB
			2 LT. BRIDGMAN and 2LT MACINTYRE rejoined from leave.	
			CSM and 1 OR rejoined from leave	MOB

(A7092). Wt. W12859/M1293. 750,000. 1/17. D. D. & L., Ltd. Forms/C.2118/14.

WAR DIARY
or
INTELLIGENCE SUMMARY

Army Form C. 2118.

Place	Date	Hour	Summary of Events and Information	Remarks and references to Appendices
HARGICOURT	18/2/18		During the day in the line a considerable increase of Hostile M.G. fire was noticed directed against our forward track. This firing was however successfully dealt with by our M.G. firing on all known enemy M.G. positions all together 7. 3rd M.G. Coy fired 41,000 rds during the night	PKep
HARGICOURT	19/2/18		An enemy M.G. was apparently quite out of action after being engaged on her emplacement by our 4 our Vickers during	MCB

Army Form C. 2118.

WAR DIARY
or
INTELLIGENCE SUMMARY.
(Erase heading not required.)

Instructions regarding War Diaries and Intelligence Summaries are contained in F.S. Regs., Part II. and the Staff Manual respectively. Title pages will be prepared in manuscript.

Place	Date	Hour	Summary of Events and Information	Remarks and references to Appendices
HARGICOURT	20/7/18		1 O.R. rejoined from Hospital.	
HARGICOURT	7/9/18		As the enemy were believed to be retiring M.G. fire was directed on all enemy tracks leading to their trenches on our front and all known tracks with a view to harassing his movements. 34000 Rounds were fired	
RONSSOY	2/9/18		17th A.A.S.Bty relieved 8 guns of 78rd M.G.Coy on 2/9/18 A.A.S.Coy relieved 3 guns of 173rd M.G.Coy. Coy H.Q. have moved to TEMPLEUX QUARRY.	

WAR DIARY
INTELLIGENCE SUMMARY

Army Form C. 2118.

Place	Date	Hour	Summary of Events and Information	Remarks and references to Appendices
TOMPIEUX QUARRY	23/4/18		73rd M.G. Coy relieved 4 guns of the 191st M.G. Coy at TOMPIEUX CEMETERY	Miles
TOMPIEUX QUARRY	24/4/18		The 3 guns of the 73rd M.G. Coy at TOMPIEUX CEMETERY were removed and placed in positions which were selected in SHERWOOD TRENCH. Open emplacements were constructed. Harassing fire was carried out during the night on enemy tracks.	
TOMPIEUX QUARRY	25/4/18		1 O.R. admitted to C.C.S. 2/Lt Peachey and 2 Lt Wells and 2 OR reinforcements from M.G.B. Depot.	

Army Form C. 2118.

WAR DIARY
or
INTELLIGENCE SUMMARY.
(Erase heading not required.)

Instructions regarding War Diaries and Intelligence Summaries are contained in F. S. Regs., Part II. and the Staff Manual respectively. Title pages will be prepared in manuscript.

Place	Date	Hour	Summary of Events and Information	Remarks and references to Appendices
TCMBLAUX QUARRY	27/9/18		4 O.R. evacuated to F.A.	W/OB
	28/9/18		"Army action." Expected enemy attack nothing happened.	(5)

Edward Field
1/3rd M.G. Coy

www.ingramcontent.com/pod-product-compliance
Lightning Source LLC
Chambersburg PA
CBHW080848230426
43662CB00013B/2050